Jesus
Recycled

The Ultimate Sustainable Resource

Compiled and Illustrated by
Elizabeth Wallace

for Lauren and Julia

"Recycled," is certainly appropriate when applied to the words of Jesus, for his teachings were "recycled" by word of mouth during his lifetime, for written accounts appeared thirty to fifty years after his death and for 2,000 years no words have been more "recycled," recorded, repeated, translated, or transcribed. Their resonating truth has proved to be an enduring "Resource," as it continues to "Sustain" 2.1 billion of the world's Christians in times of hope, struggle, joy, and despair.

TABLE OF CONTENTS

Preface

In AD 180 Bishop Irenaeus of Gaul (now Lyons, France) faced the challenge of selecting four gospels out of the hundreds that circulated throughout Europe, Greece, Egypt, and Asia Minor. At a time when the earth was considered flat, and therefore had four corners, he chose four gospels: Matthew, Mark, Luke, and John. Bishop Irenaeus wrote, "There are four winds, four directions on the compass, four elements, and four pillars of the church, therefore there must be four gospels." He mentions many of the discarded gospels by name, in particular those of Thomas, Philip, Judas, and Mary Magdalene. By his very account we know that they existed.

In AD 318 Rome ceased its persecution of the followers of Jesus, called the Christ. Seven years later the Roman Emperor Constantine held council in Nicea (present day Iznik, Turkey) to unite the many Christian sects in Europe and establish a uniform doctrine under the Roman Empire.

The primary objective of the council was to determine the spiritual versus the terrestrial essence of the Israelite they called Jesus and his relation to the Creator/Father.

Any connection of Jesus to the feminine was set only in terms of salvation, since the feminine was associated with the fallen world of procreation and original sin. (In AD 591 Pope Gregory the Great drew the moral conclusion that Mary Magdalene was not an apostle and teacher who was close to Jesus but a repentant prostitute. In 1969 the Second Vatican Council apologetically removed this label, which had debased her memory for close to 1,500 years.)

The Council of Nicea placed Jesus as a uniquely divine incarnation with the Church of Rome as his representative. Pope, bishops and priests became Christ on earth, omnipotent intermediaries between humankind and Father God.

Central to the goal of establishing a unified church was the extermination of the many Gnostic sects whose precepts were arrived at through intuition and the knowledge of self through transcendence. Such an intangible could not be harnessed by an institutional oligarchy. The danger of Gnosticism was that "inner knowing" negated the need for a conduit, i.e., an authoritarian church. Furthermore, some Gnostic Gospels portrayed Mary Magdalene's position in the life of Jesus as that of intimate consort. As Gnosticism did not possess an effective system of organization, for it is a solitary path, it was no match for the military forces of Rome. Gnosticism was annihilated.

In 1945 twelve leather-bound papyrus codices containing fifty-two Gnostic treatises were found in Nag Hammadi, Northern Egypt; a discovery that altered established precepts of Christian doctrine for all time. Why were these manuscripts, along with that of the Gospel of Judas, delayed in reaching the public for so many years?

Unlike the Dead Sea Scrolls, discovered the same year, the Nag Hammadi codices were ensnared in greed and political battles: antiquities dealers trying to get rich, political roadblocks, and the competitive atmosphere of academia. The Jung Foundation in Zürich, Switzerland bought twelve codices in 1952 and stored them in a safe-deposit box. In 1961 UNESCO (United Nations Educational, Scientific and Cultural Organization) intervened, setting up a committee to arrange publication. The Nag Hammadi documents finally came into the public domain in the 1970's, inspiring Dr. Elaine Pagels, Princeton historian of religion, to write the 1979 bestseller, *The Gnostic Gospels*.

The Gospel of Judas, discovered in 1978, was plagued by the same dynamics that hindered the Nag Hammadi codices: traded on the antiquities market for decades, stashed in a safe deposit box in New York for sixteen years, and eventually rescued by art scholars at the turn of the twenty-first century.

Selected quotes from the Gnostic Gospels of Thomas, Philip, Mary Magdalene, and Judas are presented here for the first time in union with the Canonical Gospels of Matthew, Mark, Luke, and John. Any words other than those of Jesus are solely for the purpose of clarification of context.

The same verse may be found quoted in more than one chapter. For example, references to *love* will be found both in the chapter "Relationship to Others" and in the chapter "Love." Quotes relative to *enlightenment* will be found in the chapter "Relationship to Self" and "Awakened Perception." References to *truth* will be found in the chapter "Anxiety" and the chapter "The Spirit of Truth," etc.

Other quotes may seem repetitive in that Mark, Matthew, and Luke, often intersect, echoing one another. They are what is referred to as the "Synoptic Gospels," the term coming from the Greek 'syn,' meaning "together," and 'optic,' meaning "seen." Scholars agree that the Gospel of Mark was written first, AD 65-80, followed by the Gospel of Matthew AD 80-100, then Gospel of Luke AD 80-130.

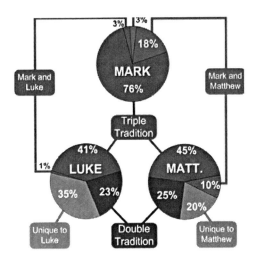

The Gospel of John, AD 90-120, is considered to be the most unique of the four and is not included as a Synoptic Gospel, although John echoes the style of Mark, and his Passion narrative resembles Luke's.

It is well known that the gospels, now preserved in historical archives, are copies of copies of copies. In the first century of the Jesus movement the tradition was oral; Mark, Matthew, Luke, and John did not write the gospels whose names they bear. Although carbon-14 dated from the second to the fourth centuries, the Nag Hammadi Papyrus and the Gospels of Judas and Mary Magdalene, are also considered to be copies of copies of copies, originating before the time of Irenaeus.

What is remarkable is that these Coptic scripts, unearthed some 1,800 years after they were banned and buried, corroborate the Canonical Gospels; a testimony to the veracity of the teachings and the life of Jesus of Nazareth.

   📖   📖   📖

In AD 180 there was a 90% illiteracy rate. Today that number stands on its head with close to a 99% literacy in North & South America, Europe and the Middle East Basin.

We can now read with an open mind.

Elizabeth Wallace

I am the light over all things.
Thomas 77

1. RELATIONSHIP TO GOD

I am the light that is over all things. I am all: from me all came forth, and to me all attained. Split a piece of wood; I am there. Lift up the stone, and you will find me there.
Thomas 77

Which of you, having a hundred sheep, if you have lost one of them, does not leave the ninety-nine in the wilderness, and go after the one which is lost, until you have found it? And when you have found it, you lay it on your shoulders, rejoicing. And when he comes home, he calls together his friends and her neighbors, saying to them, "Rejoice with me, for I have found my sheep which was lost." Just so, I tell you, there will be more joy in heaven over one person who finds their way than over ninety-nine righteous persons who need no forgiveness.
> Jesus speaks to the Pharisees who accused him of mingling with sinners, reminding them that all are of immeasurable value,
> *Luke* 15:4-7

The exiled will return to unity and be fulfilled.
Philip

Our relationship to God is like a shepherd who had a hundred sheep. One of them, the largest, went astray. He left the ninety-nine and looked for the one until he found it. After his toil, he said to the sheep, "I love you more than the ninety-nine."
Thomas 107

Images are visible to people, but the light within them is hidden in the image of the Father's light. He will be disclosed, but His image is hidden by His light.
Thomas 83

There was a man who had two sons. The younger of them said to his father, "Father, give me the share of property that

3

falls to me." And he divided his living between them. Not many days later, the younger son gathered all he had and took his journey into a far country, and there he squandered his property in loose living. And when he had spent everything, a great famine arose in that country, and he had nothing left. So he went and joined himself to one of the citizens of that country who sent him into his fields to feed pigs. And he would gladly have fed on the pods that those swine ate; and no one gave him anything. But when he came to himself he said, "How many of my father's hired servants have bread enough to spare, but I perish here with hunger! I will get up and go to my father, and I will say to him, 'Father, I have wronged heaven and you; I am no longer worthy to be called your son; treat me as one of your hired servants.'" And he got up and went to his father. But while he was yet at a distance his father saw him and had compassion and ran and embraced him and kissed him. And the son said to him, "Father, I have wronged heaven and I have wronged you; I am no longer worthy to be called your son."

But the father said to his servants, "Bring quickly the best robe, and put it on him; and put a ring on his hand, and shoes on his feet; and bring the fatted calf and kill it, and let us eat and be merry; for this son of mine was dead, and is alive again; he was lost, and now he is found." And they began to celebrate.

Now his elder son was in the field; and as he came and drew near to the house, he heard music and dancing. And he called one of the servants and asked what this meant. And he said to him, "Your brother has come, and your father has killed the fatted calf, because he has received him safe and sound." But he was angry and refused to go in.

His father came out and asked him to join them, but he answered his father, "Look, all these years I have served you and I never disobeyed your command; yet you never gave me a calf that I might celebrate with my friends. But when this son of yours came, who has devoured your living with prostitutes, you killed the fatted calf for him!"

And he said to his son, "Son, you are always with me, and all that is mine is yours. It was fitting to celebrate and be glad, for this is your brother who was dead and is alive; he was lost and now he is found."

Jesus explains to the Pharisees and scribes of the Temple why he ate with sinners and tax collectors, *Luke* 15:11-32

I am the true vine and my Father, the source of all life, tends to the vines. Every branch of mine that bears no fruit is taken away, and every branch that does bear fruit is pruned that it may bear more fruit. You are already renewed by the words that I have spoken to you. Abide in me, and I in you. As the branch cannot bear fruit by itself unless it abides in the vine, neither can you, unless you abide in me. I am the vine, you are the branches. Who ever abides in me will bear much fruit, for apart from me you can do nothing.

Speaking to the twelve at the Passover Supper, *John* 15:1-5

If one does not abide in me, he is cast forth as a branch and withers; and the branches are gathered, thrown into the fire and burned. If you live in me and my words live in you, ask whatever you will and it will be done for you. By this the Father is glorified, that you bear much fruit and so prove to be my followers.

Jesus speaks to his disciples at the Last Supper on remaining connected to the source of life, *John* 15:6-8

Truly, truly, I say to you, before Abraham was, I am.

The Jews ask Jesus if he has seen Abraham. He responds stating the infinite presence of the divine, *John* 8:58

The Father and I are one.

In answer to the people of Israel who question whether Jesus is demon or deity, *John* 10:30

I who speak to you am he .

Jesus reveals that he is the promised one to the
Samaritan woman by the well, *John* 4:26

I am; and you will see the Son of Man sitting at the right
hand of the Father, and coming with the clouds of heaven.

At his trial Jesus states to Pilot that he *is* the Son of God,
Mark 14:62

The dark powers imagine it is by their own self-will that they
do what they do, yet the Holy Spirit secretly does all through
them, as it wills.

Philip

When you have lifted up the Son of Man then you will know
that I am He and that I do nothing on my own authority but
speak as the Father taught me. And He who sent me is with
me. He has not left me alone, for I always do His will.

Jesus clarifies his purpose to the Jews who question his
identity as the instrument of the Creator, *John* 10:17-18

Whoever receives you receives me, and whoever receives me
receives the one who sent me.

Speaking to his followers as he declares them to be messengers
of a higher source, *Matthew* 10:40

It is written, "You shall worship the Lord your God and Him
only shall you serve."

Resisting the temptation of Satan, *Luke* 4:8

So everyone who acknowledges me before Man, I also will
acknowledge before my Father who is in heaven, but
whoever denies me before Man, I also will deny before my
Father who is in heaven.

Matthew 10:32-33

A grapevine has been planted apart from the Father. Since it is not strong, it will be pulled up by its root and will perish.
Thomas 40

A man once gave a great banquet and invited many; and at the time for the banquet he sent his servant to say to those who had been invited, "Come, for all is now ready." But they all alike began to make excuses. The first said to him, "I have bought a field, and I must go out and see it; I pray you, have me excused." And another said, "I have bought five yoke of oxen, and I go to examine them; I pray you, have me excused." And another said, "I have married a wife, and therefore I cannot come." So the servant came and reported this to his master. Then the householder in anger said to him servant, "Go out quickly to the streets and lanes of the city, and bring in the poor and maimed and blind and lame." And the servant said, "Sir, what you commanded has been done and still there is room." And the master said to the servant, "Go out to the highways and hedges, and compel people to come in, that my house may be filled. For I tell you, none of those men who were invited shall taste my banquet."

> At the Passover Supper Jesus speaks about the table of life and the Creator's longing for it to be filled,
> *Luke* 14:16-24, *Thomas* 64

And when you fast do not look dismal like the hypocrites, for they disfigure their faces that their fasting may be seen by others. Truly, I say to you, they have their reward. But when you fast, anoint your head and wash your face that your fasting may not be seen by others but by your Father who is in secret; and your Father who sees in secret will reward you.

> Sermon on the Mount, *Matthew* 6:16-18

Whoever hears you hears me and whoever rejects you rejects me and whoever rejects me rejects the Father who sent me.

> Jesus appointed 70 others to go before him into every city,
> *Luke* 10:16

7

And I tell you, everyone who acknowledges me before others, the Son of Man also will acknowledge before the angels of God, but those who deny me will be denied before the angels of God.

Luke 12:8-9

Truly I say to you, all sins will be forgiven the sons and daughters of humanity, and whatever blasphemies they utter, but whoever blasphemes against the Holy Spirit never has forgiveness, but is guilty of an eternal sin.

Responding to those who accused him of working with the devil, *Mark* 3:28-29

But I know that you have not the love of God within you. I have come in the name of my Father, and you do not receive me, if another comes in his own name, him you will receive. How can you believe, who receive glory from one another and do not seek the glory that comes from the only God?

Jesus responds to those in power who persecute him,
John 5:42-44

It is written, "You shall not live by bread alone, but by every word that proceeds from the mouth of God."

Jesus' response to the temptations of Satan after fasting 40 days,
Matthew 4:4, *Luke* 4:4

I am not laughing at you. <You> are not doing this of your own will but because it is through this that your god [will be] praised.

Jesus responds to the disciples who question why He laughs at their pious prayer of thanksgiving over the bread. *Judas*

Why has this agitation led you to anger? Your god who is within you and [...] [35] have provoked you to anger [within] your soul. [Let] any one of you who is [strong enough] among human beings bring out the perfect human and stand before my face.

Observing their lack of understanding, Jesus challenges the disciples. Judas stands in humility, with eyes lowered. *Judas*

And do not fear those who kill the body but cannot kill the soul. But rather fear Him who is able to destroy both soul and body in hell.

Matthew 10:28, *Luke* 12:4-5

I tell you, if my followers were silent, the very stones would cry out.

Jesus responds to the Pharisees who urge him to silence his followers, *Luke* 19:40

O Jerusalem, Jerusalem, killing the prophets, and stoning those sent to you. How often would I have gathered your children together as a hen gathers her chicks under her wings, but you would not.

Matthew 23:37

Call no one on earth 'father;' you have but one Father in heaven."

Matthew 23:9

And this is eternal life, that they many know You, the only true God, and Jesus Christ whom you have sent.

John 17:3

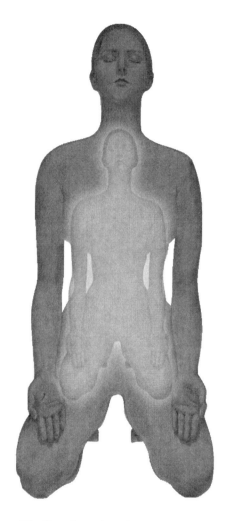

The Kingdom of God is within you.
Luke 17:20-21

2. RELATIONSHIP TO SELF

If you bring forth what is within you, what you bring forth will save you. If you do not bring forth what is within you, what you do not bring forth [will] destroy you.
Thomas 70

There's a perfect light at the heart of a man or woman of light that lights up the whole world. If the light fails to shine, there's darkness.
Thomas 24

If you are whole, you will be filled with light, but if you are divided, you will be filled with darkness.
Thomas 61

When you make the two into one, you will become children of Adam, and when you say, "Mountain, move from here!" it will move.
Thomas 106

I tell you that the child is within you all! Seek the child inside; those who search diligently and earnestly shall surely find [it].
Jesus speaks to his followers, *Mary Magdalene*

Why do you wash the outside of the cup? Don't you understand that the one who made the inside is also the one who made the outside?
Thomas 89

It is needed to own the All, to know one's Self. If one doesn't know one's Self it's impossible to enjoy what is owned. Those who've come to know themselves enjoy what they own.
Philip

Woe to you, scribes and Pharisees, hypocrites! For you cleanse the outside of the cup and dish, but inside you are full of extortion and self-indulgence. Blind Pharisee, first cleanse the inside of the cup and dish, that the outside of them may be clean also.

Speaking to the multitudes on the same theme,
Matthew 23:25-26

Each one of us must dig down deep within ourselves and find the root of this evil egotism in the heart so it will perish. If we ignore this root, more poisonous fruit is produced in the heart; it becomes our taskmaster and enslaves us, forcing us to do what it desires.

Philip

The worldly see the All but fail to know their own Self; through Truth you learn to know your Self; what you know, you become.

Philip

Those who know all but are lacking in themselves, are utterly lacking

Thomas 67

If those who lead you say to you, "See, the kingdom is in the sky," then the birds of the sky will precede you. If they say to you, "It is in the sea," then the fish will precede you. Rather, the kingdom is inside of you, and it is outside of you. When you come to know yourselves, then you will become known, and you will realize that it is you who are sons and daughters of the living God. But if you will not know yourselves, you dwell in poverty and it is you who are that poverty.

Thomas 3

The kingdom of God is not coming with signs to be observed; nor will they say, "Lo, here it is!" or "There!" for behold, the kingdom of God is within you.

Jesus' response to the Pharisees when asked when the kingdom would come, *Luke* 17:20-21

Beware that no one lead you astray saying Lo here or lo there! For the Son of Man is within you.

Mary Magdalene 4:34

Which of you, desiring to build a tower, does not first sit down and count the cost, whether he has enough to complete it? Otherwise, when he has laid a foundation and is not able to finish, all who see it begin to mock him, saying, "This man began to build and was not able to finish."

Luke 14:28-30

If a kingdom is divided against itself, that kingdom cannot stand.

Responding to the scribes and Pharisees who accused him of being one with the devil, Mark 3:24

Every kingdom divided against itself is laid waste, and no city or house divided against itself will stand.

On the same theme, Matthew 12:25

Who has great faith in truth has found the real life; this one dares dying to the Self to be truly alive.

Philip

Truly I say to you, unless one is born anew he cannot see the kingdom of God.

Jesus speaks to Nicodemus, a man of the Pharisees who believed that Jesus was a man of God, John 3:3

To the great he seemed great, to the little he was little, to the angels he was an angel, to men he was a man. So his Word was hidden from all; some indeed saw him and imagined they were seeing themselves.

Philip

When you make the two into one, and when you make the inner like the outer and the outer line the inner, and the upper like the lower, and when you make male and female into a single one, so that the male will not be male nor the female be female…then you will enter the kingdom.

Thomas 22

I am the one who comes from what is undivided…for this reason I say, whoever is [undivided] will be full of light, but whoever is divided will be full of darkness.

Thomas 61

You are the light of the world. A city that is set on a hill cannot be hidden. Not do they light a lamp and put it under a basked, but on a lamp stand, and it gives light to all who are in the house. Let your light so shine before men, they may see your good works and glorify your father in heaven.

Matthew 5: 14-16

If two make peace...they will say to the mountain,
"Move from here!" and it will move.
Thomas: 48

3. RELATIONSHIP TO OTHERS

If your brother sins against you, go and tell him his fault between the two of you alone. If he listens to you, you have gained your brother. But if he does not listen, take one or two others along with you that the evidence of two or three witnesses may confirm every word. If he refuses to listen to them, tell it to the church; and if he refuses to listen even to the church, let him be to you as a Gentile and a tax collector.

Jesus responds to his disciples when they ask, "Who is the greatest in the Kingdom of Heaven?" *Matthew* 18:15-17

A new commandment I give you, that you love one another; even as I have loved you, that you also love one another. By this all will know that you are my disciples, if you have love for one another.

Final words at the Passover Supper, *John* 13:34-35

Father forgive them, for they know not what they do.

On the cross Jesus expresses complete understanding of the human condition, *Luke* 23:34

If you are offering your gift at the altar and there remember that your brother or sister has something against you, leave your gift there before the altar and go; first be reconciled to your brother or sister and then come and offer your gift.

From the Sermon on the Mount, *Matthew* 5:23-24

For truly, I say to you that whoever gives you a cup of water to drink because you bear the name of Christ, will by no means lose their reward.

Mark 9:41

"For I was hungry and you gave me food, I was thirsty and you gave me drink, I was a stranger and you welcomed me, I was naked and you clothed me, I was sick and you visited me, I was in prison and you came to me."

Then the disciples answered him, "Lord, when did we see you hungry and feed you, or thirsty and give you to drink? And when did we see you as a stranger and welcome you, or naked and clothe you? And when did we see you sick or in prison and visit you?"
And Jesus answered them, "Truly I say to you, as you did it to one of the least of these my brothers and sisters, you did it to me."

> Jesus explains to his disciples that we are all children from the same Creator, *Matthew* 25:35-40

Then he will say to those at his left hand, "Depart from me you cursed, into the eternal fire prepared for the devil and his followers. For I was hungry and you gave me no food, I was thirsty and you gave me no drink, I was a stranger and you did not welcome me, naked and you did not clothe me, sick and in prison and you did not visit me."

> On the same theme, *Matthew* 25:41-43

Do not give dogs what is holy and do not throw your pearls before swine, lest they trample them under foot and turn to attack you.

> From the Sermon on the Mount, *Matthew* 7:6

Do not give what is holy to dogs, or they might throw them upon the manure pile. Do not throw pearls [to] swine, or they might make [mud] of it.

> *Thomas* 93

A man was going down from Jerusalem to Jericho, and he fell among robbers, who stripped him and beat him, and departed, leaving him half-dead. Now by chance a priest was going down the road; and when he saw him he passed by on the other side. So likewise a Levite, when he came to the place and saw him, passed by on the other side. But a Samaritan, as he journeyed, came to where he was; and when he saw him he had compassion and went to him and bound up his wounds, pouring on oil and wine; then he set him on his own beast and brought him to an inn and took care of him. And the next day he took out two denarii and gave them to the innkeeper saying, "Take care of him; and whatever more you spend, I will repay you when I come back." Which of these three, do you think, proved neighbor to the man who fell among the robbers?

> A lawyer questions Jesus asking him to define the word "neighbor." Jesus gives the example of a Samarian stating that we must help one another regardless of race or belief,
> *Luke* 10:30-37

"You wicked servant! I forgave you all that debt because you besought me; and shouldn't you forgive the debt of your fellow servant, as I had mercy on you?" And in anger his lord delivered him to the jailers, until he paid all of his debt. So also your heavenly Father will do to every one of you, if you do not forgive your brother and sister from your heart.

> *Matthew* 18:32-35

I do not say to you that you should forgive seven times, but seventy times seven.

> *Matthew* 18:22

If your sister or brother sins, speak to them, and if they say they are sorry, forgive them; and if they sin against you seven times in one day, and turn to you seven times and say, "I'm sorry," you must forgive.

> On the same theme, *Luke* 17: 3-4

For if you forgive others of their wrongdoings, your Father in heaven will also forgive you; but if you do not forgive others their trespasses, neither will your Father forgive you.

> From the Sermon on the Mount, *Matthew* 6:14-15

…who reaps receives wages, and gathers fruit for eternal life, so that sower and reaper may rejoice together. For here the saying holds true, "One sows and another reaps." I sent you to reap that for which you did not labor. Others have labored, and you have entered into their labor.

When the disciples ask if Jesus has been fed, he speaks to them of the food of life, *John* 4:36-38

The first commandment is, "Hear, O Israel: the Lord our God, the Lord is one: and you shall love the Lord your God with all your heart, and with all your soul, and with all your mind, and with all your strength." The second is this, "You shall love your neighbor as yourself." There is no other commandment greater then these.

Speaking to the scribe of the two simple rules, *Mark* 12:29-31

But I say to you that hear, love your enemies, do good to those who hate you, bless those who curse you, pray for those who abuse you. To him who strikes you on the cheek, offer the other also; and from him who takes away your cloak do not withhold your coat as well. Give to every one who begs from you, and of those who take away your goods do not ask them again. And as you wish that others would do to you, do so to them. If you love those who love you, what credit is that to you? For even sinners love those who love them. And if you do good to those who do good to you, what credit is that to you? For even wrongdoers do the same. And if you lend to those from whom you hope to receive, what credit is that to you? Even evildoers lend to sinners, to receive as much again. But love your enemies, and do good, and lend, expecting nothing in return; and your reward will be great, and you will be sons and daughters of the Most High; for our creator is kind to the ungrateful and the selfish. Be merciful, even as your Creator is merciful.

From the Sermon on the Mount, *Luke* 6:27-36

You have heard that it was said, "You shall love your neighbor and hate your enemy." But I say to you, love your enemies and pray for those who persecute you, so that you may be sons and daughters of the source of all love who is in heaven; for the sun rises on the evil and on the good, and rain falls on the just and on the unjust. For if you love those who love you, what reward have you? Do not even the tax collectors do the same? And if you salute only your friends, what more are you doing than anyone else? Do not even the Gentiles do the same? You, therefore, must be perfect, as your Father in heaven is perfect.

> On the same these from the Sermon on the Mount,
> *Matthew* 5:43-48

Do you know what I have done to you? You call me Rabbi and Lord; and you are right, for so I am. If I then, your Lord and Rabbi, has washed your feet, you also ought to wash one another's feet. For I have given you an example, that you also should do as I have done to you. Truly, truly I say to you, a servant is not greater than his master, nor is he who is sent greater than he who sent him. If you know these things, blessed are you if you do them.

> After Jesus has washed the feet of his disciples he speaks of
> service to one another, *John* 13:12-17

Peace be with you. As the Father has sent me, even so I send you. …Receive the Holy Spirit. If you forgive the sins of anyone, they are forgiven; if you retain the sins of anyone, they are retained.

> Jesus appears to Mary Magdalene and the twelve after the
> crucifixion instructing that in forgiveness there is release and in
> release there is peace, *John* 20:21-23

If two make peace with each other in a single house, they will say to the mountain, "Move from here!" and it will move.

> *Thomas* 48

He that is not against you is for you.

> *Luke* 9:50

Have you not read that the Creator who made them from the beginning made them male and female and said, "For this reason a man shall leave his father and mother and be joined to his wife and the two shall become one?" So they are no longer two but one. What therefore God has joined together let no one put asunder.

Christ responds to the Pharisees as they question him on marriage, *Matthew* 19:4-6

Every one who divorces his wife and marries another commits adultery and he who marries a woman divorced from her husband commits adultery.

To the Pharisees on the same theme, *Luke* 16:18

For your hardness of heart he wrote you this commandment (Moses allowed divorce). But from the beginning of creation God made them male and female. For this reason a man shall leave his father and mother and be joined to his wife and the two shall become one. So they are no longer two but one. What God has joined together let not man put asunder…Whoever divorces his wife and marries another, commits adultery against her; and if she divorces her husband and marries another, she commits adultery.

Jesus responds to both the Pharisees and his disciples in the same manner, *Mark* 10:5-12

When revealed, the perfect light will shine on all.
Philip

4. DARK & LIGHT

Light and darkness, life and death, right and left, are inseparable twins. For the good are not wholly good nor the wicked wholly wicked, nor is life merely life, nor death merely death; each will return to its primal source.

Philip

Whatever you have spoken in the dark will be heard in the light, and what you have spoken in the ear in inner rooms will be proclaimed on the housetops.

Luke 12:3

There is no sin in reality! It is you who create sin, when you do deeds, such as fornication, that are called sinful. That is why the Good came into your midst, to the essence of every nature in order to restore it to its root. …

Mary Magdalene 4:26-28

The dark powers imagine it is by their own self-will that they do what they do; yet the Holy Spirit secretly does all through them, as it wills.

Philip

When you rid yourselves of guilt and shame and tear off your old rags and trample them beneath your feet like children. Then you'll see the son of he who is the living God, and you'll never need fear again.

Thomas

I am the one who comes from what is undivided…for this reason I say, whoever is [undivided] will be full of light, but whoever is divided will be full of darkness.

Thomas 61

What comes out of a man is what defiles a man. For from within, out of the heart of man come evil thoughts, fornication, theft, murder, adultery, coveting, wickedness, deceit, licentiousness, envy, slander, pride, foolishness. All these evil things come from within and they defile a man.

Jesus explains to his disciples that they will be known by their deeds, Mark 7:20-23

When a blind and sighted man are both in darkness, they are equal. When light dawns, he who can see will know the light; he who is blind will stay in the dark.

Jesus explains the vision of understanding, *Philip*

Truly, truly I say to you, every one who commits sin is a slave to sin. The slave does not continue in the house forever; the son continues forever. So if the truth makes you free, you will be free indeed.

Jesus speaks to the Pharisees in the treasury, *John* 8:34-36

There's a perfect light at the heart of a man or woman of light that lights up the whole world. If they fail to shine, there's darkness.

Thomas 24

When revealed, the perfect light will shine on all; all those within its rays will be anointed and receive baptism of the chrism.

Philip

When the unclean spirit has gone out of a person, it passes through waterless places seeking rest, but it finds none. Then it says, "I will return to my house from which I came." And when it comes it finds the house empty, swept, and put in order. Then it goes and brings with it seven other spirits more evil than itself, and they enter and dwell there; and the last state of that person becomes worse than the first. So shall it be also with the evil of this generation.

Speaking to the scribes and Pharisees,
Matthew 12:43-45

Images are visible to people, but the light within them is hidden in the image of the Father's light. He will be disclosed, but his image is hidden by his light.
Thomas 83

Truly, truly I say to you, every one who commits sin is a slave to sin. The slave does not continue in the house forever; the child continues forever. So if the truth makes you free, you will be free indeed.
John 8:34-36

In the world there's good and evil. Its goodness is not wholly good, nor is its evil wholly evil. But there's an evil that is diabolic, this "in betweenness."
On noncommittal mediocrity, *Philip*

Get behind me Satan! You are a hindrance to me, for you are not on the side of God but of men.
A comment to Peter when he made a wrong choice,
Matthew 16:23

Get behind me, Satan! For you are not on the side of God, but of man.
Mark 8:33

Begone Satan! For it is written, "You shall worship the Lord your God and Him only shall you serve."
When Jesus was confronted by Satan, *Matthew* 4:10

If you are whole, you will be filled with light, but if you are divided, you will be filled with darkness.
Thomas 61

The light is with you for a little longer. Walk in the light while you have the light, lest the darkness overtake you. Those who walk in darkness do not know where they go. While you have the light, believe in the light that you may become children of the light.

> On the light of consciousness, *John* 12:35-36

No one after lighting a lamp puts it in a cellar or under a bushel, but on a stand that those who enter may see the light. Your eye is the lamp of your body. When your eye is sound, your whole body is full of light. But when it is not sound, your body is full of darkness. Therefore be careful lest the light in you be darkness. If then your whole body is full of light, having no part dark, it will be wholly bright as when a lamp with its rays gives you light.

> *Luke* 11:33-36

What you will hear in your ear, in the other ear proclaim from your rooftops. For no one lights a lamp and puts it under a basket, nor does one put it in a hidden place. Rather, one puts it on a lamp stand so that all who come and go will see its light.

> *Thomas* 33

You are the light of the world. A city set on a hill cannot be hid. Nor do people light a lamp and put it under a bushel, but on a stand, and it gives light to all in the house. Let your light so shine before the world, that all may see your good works and give glory to your Father who is in heaven.

> In the Sermon on the Mount Jesus speaks of the need for our light to shine in the world, *Matthew* 5:14-16

If any one walks in the day, they do not stumble because they see the light of this world. But if any one walks in the night, they stumble because the light is not in them.

> *John* 11:9-10

You could have no power at all against me unless it had been given you from above.

John 19:11, Jesus responds to Pilate who said, "Do you not know that I have the power to crucify you and to release you?"

What I tell you in darkness, speak in the light; and hear in the ear, proclaim from the housetops.

Matthew 10:27

If anyone becomes a child of the light he will receive the light. If anyone does not receive it while he is here, he will not be able to receive it in the other place.

Philip

29

Whoever does the will of God
is my brother and sister and mother.
Mark 3:35

5. FAMILY

Who are my mother and my brethren? Here are my mother and my brethren! Whoever does the will of God is my brother and sister and mother.

> Jesus responds to those who say his mother and brothers are looking for him, *Mark* 3:33-35

All those here who do the will of my Father are my mother and brothers and sisters; they're the ones who will enter the Kingdom of Heaven.

> *Thomas*

He who does not reject his mother and father, because of my teaching, will not become my disciple. For my mother gave me birth, but my real Mother gave me life.

> *Thomas*

If any one comes to me and does not hate his own father and mother and wife and children and brothers and sisters, yes and even his own life, he cannot be my disciple. If you do not bear your own cross and come after me, you cannot be my disciple.

> Jesus speaks to the multitudes about rejecting parents who do not follow the path of truth, *Luke* 14:27-27

Those who crave to be heirs of the dead, are already spiritually dead and will inherit death. Those who seek to be heirs of the living, are spiritually alive, and will inherit what is both alive and dead. The dead inherit nothing, yet if they inherit what is living, they'll gain Eternal Life.

> *Philip*

If God were your Father, you would love me, for I proceeded forth and came from God nor have I come of myself. He sent me. Why do you not understand my words? Because you are not able to listen. You are the father of the devil, and the desires of your father you want to do. He was a murderer from the beginning, and has nothing to do with the truth, because there is no truth in him. When he lies, he speaks according to his own nature, for he is a liar and the source of lies.

> Jesus responds to the Pharisees who question his legitimacy saying, "We were not born of fornication," *John* 8:42-44

Truly, truly, I say to you, unless one is born of water and the Spirit, you cannot enter the kingdom of God. That which is born of the flesh is flesh, and that which is born of the Spirit is spirit. Do not marvel that I say to you, "You must be born anew." The wind blows where it wishes, and you hear the sound of it, but you do not know where it comes or where it goes. So it is with every one who is born of the Spirit.

> Nicodemus questions the possibility of a second birth, *John* 3:5-8

If you're born a man or a woman, a human being will love you; if you become truly spiritual, the spirit will love you.

> *Philip*

Truly I say to you, there is no one who has left house or brothers or sisters or mother or father or children or lands for my sake and for the sake of the gospel who will not receive a hundred fold now in this time, houses and brothers and sisters and mothers and children and lands, with persecutions and in the age to come, eternal life.

> Speaking to Peter of the lineage of spirit, *Mark* 10:29-30

Those of you who love father or mother more than me is not worthy of me; and those of you who love son or daughter more than me is not worthy of me.

> The spirit of truth as the core of relationships, *Matthew* 10:37

Whoever does not hate father and mother cannot be my disciple, and whoever does not hate brothers and sisters, and carry the cross as I do, will not be worthy of me.

On the same theme, *Thomas* 55

She has done a beautiful thing...
Mark 14

6. MARY MAGDALENE

Peter said to Mary, "Sister we know that the Savior loved you more than the rest of women. Tell us his words that you remember, those we've never heard before."
Mary Magdalene 5:5

Peter said, "Did He really speak privately with a woman and not openly to us? Are we to turn about and all listen to her? Did He prefer her to us?"
Then Mary wept and said to Peter, "My brother Peter, what do you think? Do you think that I have thought this up myself in my heart, or that I am lying about the Savior?"
Levi answered and said to Peter, "Peter you have always been hot tempered. Now I see you contending against the woman like the adversaries. But if the Savior made her worthy, who are you indeed to reject her? Surely the Savior knows her very well. That is why he loved her more than us."
Mary Magdalene 9:4-9

You thirteenth spirit, why do you try so hard?…
Judas said, "In the vision I saw myself as the twelve disciples were stoning me and [45] persecuting [me severely]."
The gospel of Judas speaks of 13 disciples, *Judas* 3

I tell you that the child is within you all! Seek the child inside; those who search diligently and earnestly shall surely find [it].
Jesus speaks to his followers, *Mary Magdalene*

Martha, you are anxious and troubled about many things; one thing is needful. Mary has chosen the good portion, which shall not be taken away from her.

Jesus explains to Martha that Mary chose to be present in the moment, *Luke* 10:41-42

Let her alone; why do you trouble her? She has done a beautiful thing to me. For you always have the poor with you and whenever you will, you can do good to them; but you will not always have me. She has done what she could; she has anointed my body beforehand for burying. And truly I say to you, wherever the gospel is preached in the whole world, what she has done will be told in memory of her.

Jesus speaks of Mary Magdalene's devotion as she anoints him with oil, *Mark* 14:6-9

Do you see this woman? I entered your house, you gave me no water for my feet, but she has wet my feet with her tears and wiped them with her hair. You gave me no kiss, but from the time I came in she has not ceased to kiss my feet. You did not anoint my head with oil, but she has anointed my feet with ointment. Therefore I tell you, her sins, which are many, are forgiven, for she loved much; but he who is forgiven little, loves little.

On the same theme, *Luke* 7:44-47

Do not weep and do not grieve nor be irresolute, for his grace will be entirely with you and will protect you. Let us praise his greatness, for he has prepared us and made us into men and women.

Mary speaks to the disciples, *Mary Magdalene* 5:2

And the companion of the [...] Mary Magdalene. [...] loved her more than all the disciples, and used to kiss her often on her mouth. The rest of the disciples [...]. They said to him "Why do you love her more than all of us?" The Savior answered and said to them, "Why do I not love you like her?

I'll guide her soul to make her as a real man, in that place which transcends the differences between the sexes, so she'll become a living spirit. For each woman who makes herself male in this way and overcomes all differences will enter the Kingdom of Heaven.

Jesus responds to Peter who says Mary should leave because a woman is not fit for life everlasting. *Thomas*

There were three who always walked with the Lord: Mary, his mother, and her sister, and Magdalene, the one who was called his companion. His sister and his mother and his companion were each a Mary.

Philip

Matter gave birth to a passion that has no equal...
Mary Magdalene: 4:30

7. STRUGGLE

Stop struggling with me. Each of you has his own star…
Judas

Matter gave birth to a passion that has no equal, which proceeded from something contrary to nature. Then there arises a disturbance in the whole body. That is why I said to you, be of good courage, and if you are discouraged be encouraged in the presence of the different forms of nature.
Mary Magdalene 4:30-31

Don't lie, and don't do what you hate, because all things are disclosed before heaven. After all, there is nothing hidden that will not be revealed, and there is nothing covered up that will remain undisclosed.
Thomas 6

Why do you sleep? Rise and pray that you many not enter into temptation.
Jesus speaks to his disciples in the Garden of Gesthemane on the need to remain aware, *Luke* 22:46

So, could you not watch with me one hour?
Matthew 26:40

It is written, "You shall not tempt the Lord your God."
Jesus responds to Satan, *Matthew* 4:7

Blessed are you poor, for yours is the kingdom of God. Blessed are you that hunger now, for you shall be satisfied. Blessed are you that weep now, for you shall laugh. Blessed are you when you are hated, and excluded and reviled, and your name is cast out as evil on account of the Son of humankind! Rejoice in that day, and leap for joy, for behold, your reward is great in heaven. For this was also done to the prophets.

From the sermon on the mountain, *Luke* 6:20-23

Let one who seeks not stop seeking until he finds. When he finds, he will be troubled. When he is troubled, he will be astonished and will rule over all.

Thomas 2

All of you will stumble this night; for it is written, "I will strike the shepherd, and the sheep will be scattered." But after I am raised up, I will go before you to Galilee.

Predicting his abandonment in the Garden of Gethsemane, *Mark* 14:27-28

Enter by the narrow gate; for the gate is wide and the way is easy that leads to destruction, and those who enter by it are many. For the gate is narrow and the way is hard that leads to life, and those who find are few.

From the Sermon on the Mount, *Matthew* 7:13-14

Strive to enter by the narrow door, for many, I tell you, will seek to enter and will not be able.

In response to one who questions who will be saved, Jesus discourages taking the easy way, *Luke*13:24

My soul is very sorrowful, even to death. Remain here and watch with me.

Asking for support in the Garden of Gesthemane, *Matthew* 26:38

No one can serve two masters; for either he will hate the one and love the other, or he will be devoted to the one and despise the other. You cannot serve God and mammon.

Matthew 6:24, *Luke* 16:13

Blessed are the poor in spirit for theirs is the kingdom of heaven.

Blessed are those who mourn, for they shall be comforted.

Blessed are the meek, for they shall inherit the earth.

Blessed are those who hunger and thirst for righteousness, for they shall be satisfied.

Blessed are the merciful, for they shall obtain mercy.

Blessed are the pure in heart, for they shall see God.

Blessed are the peacemakers, for they shall be called children of God.

Blessed are those who are persecuted for righteousness' sake, for theirs is the kingdom of heaven.

Blessed are you when men revile you and persecute you and utter all kinds of evil against you falsely on my account. Rejoice and be glad, for your reward is great in heaven, for so men persecuted the prophets who were before you.

Sermon on the mountain, *Matthew* 5:3-12

If the world hates you, know that it has hated me before it hated you. If you were of the world, the world would love its own. Yet because you are not of the world, and I chose you out of the world, the world hates you. Remember the word that I said to you, "A servant is not greater than his master." If they persecuted me, they will persecute you; if they kept my word, they will keep yours also. But all this they will do to you on my account, because they do not know Him who sent me. If I had not come and spoken to them, they would not have sin; but now they have no excuse for their sin. He who hates me hates the Father also. If I had not done among them the works which no one else did, they would not have sin; but now they have seen and hated both me and the Father. It is to fulfill the word that is written in their law. "They hated me without a cause."

At the Passover Supper, *John* 15:18-25

The hour is coming, indeed it has come, when you will be scattered, every one to his or her own home, and will leave me alone; yet I am not alone, for the Father is with me. I have said this to you, that in me you may have peace. In the world you have tribulation. Be of good cheer, I have overcome the world.

Before the crucifixion, *John* 16:32-33

If any one would come after me, let them deny themselves and take their cross and follow me. For whoever would save their life will lose it, and whoever loses their life for my sake will find it. For what will it profit a woman or man if they gain the whole world and lose their soul? Or what shall one give in return for their life? For the Son of humankind is come with his angels in the glory of his Father, and then he will repay every man and woman for what they have done.

Self-sacrifice for the ultimate good, *Matthew* 16:24-27

But take heed to yourselves that your hearts be weighed down with dissipation and drunkenness and the cares of this life, and that day come upon you suddenly like a snare.

Luke 21:34

Take heed what you hear; the measure you give will be the measure you get and still more will be given you. For to those who have will more be given and from those who have not, even what they have will be taken away.

The growth of those who use the gifts that they have,
Mark 4:24-25

Where the body is, there the eagles will be gathered together.

At the mercy of the human condition, *Luke* 17:37

When the unclean spirit has gone out of a person, it passes through waterless places seeking rest, but it finds none. Then it says, "I will return to my house from which I came." And when it comes it finds the house empty, swept, and put in order. Then it goes and brings with it seven other spirits more evil than itself, and they enter and dwell there; and the last state of that person becomes worse than the first. So shall it be also with the evil of this generation.

Matthew 12:43-45

When the unclean spirit has gone out of a man it passes through waterless places seeking rest, and finding none it says, "I will return to my house from which I came." And when the unclean spirit comes it finds the house swept and put in order. Then it goes and brings seven other spirits more evil and they enter and dwell there, and the last state of that man becomes worse than the first.

Jesus speaks to those who said he cast out a demon in the name of Beelzebub (the devil), *Luke* 11:24-26

You will all fall away because of me this night; for it is written, "I will strike the shepherd and the sheep of the flock will be scattered."

Jesus' followers flee when he is taken prisoner, *Matthew* 26:31

Watch and pray lest you enter into temptation. The spirit indeed is willing, but the flesh is weak.

Matthew 26:41

Blessed are you who are solitary and chosen, for you will find the kingdom. Blessed in the one who has suffered and has found life.

Thomas 49 & 58

By your endurance you will gain your lives.

Luke 21:19

Holy Father... I do not pray that You should keep them out of the world, but that You should keep them from the evil one.

John 15-17

He who endures to the end will be saved.

Mark 13:13

Do not fret from morning to evening...
Thomas 36

8. ANXIETY

Do not fret from morning to evening and from evening to morning, [about your food--what you're going to eat, or about your clothing--] what you are going to wear. [You're much better than the lilies, which neither card nor spin. As for you, when you have no garment, what will you put on? Who might add to your stature? That very one will give you your garment.]

Thomas 36

Therefore I tell you, do not be anxious about your life, what you shall eat or what you shall drink, nor about your body, what you shall put on. Is not life more than food and the body more than clothing? Look at the birds of the air; they neither sow nor reap nor gather into barns, and yet your heavenly Father feeds them. Are you not of more value than they?

Matthew 6:25-26

...do not be anxious beforehand what you are to say; but say whatever is given you in that hour, for it is not you who speak, but the Spirit of Truth.

Mark 13:11

And why are you anxious about clothing? Consider the lilies of the field, how they grow; they neither toil nor spin; yet I tell you, even Solomon in all his glory was not arrayed like one of these. But if God so clothes the grass of the field, which today is alive and tomorrow is thrown into the oven, will He not much more clothe you, oh woman of little faith? Therefore do not be anxious, saying, "What shall we eat?" or "What shall we drink?" For your heavenly Father knows that you need all these things. But seek first the kingdom of God and its truth, and all these things shall be yours too Therefore do not be anxious about tomorrow, for tomorrow

will be anxious for itself. Let the day's own trouble be
sufficient for the day.

From the Sermon on the Mount, *Matthew* 6:28-34

My God, my God, why have you abandoned me?

Jesus on the cross, *Mark* 15:34

Why are you afraid? Have you no faith?

Jesus calms the disciples in a storm at sea, *Mark* 4:40

Do not fear, only believe.

Jesus speaks of healing through faith, *Mark* 5:36

Take heart, it is I; have no fear.

Matthew 14:27

I will not leave you desolate: I will come to you. Yet a
little while, and the world will see me no more, but you will
see me; because I live, you will live also. In that day you will
know that I am in my Father, and you in me, and I in you.

John 14:18-20

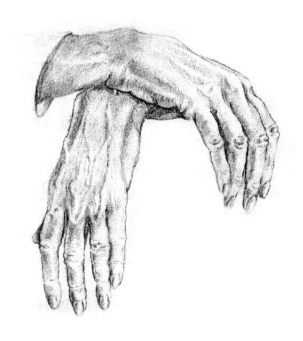

... have faith and never doubt...
Matthew 21:21

9. FAITH

Oh man of little faith, why did you doubt?
> To Peter when he became discouraged, *Matthew* 14:31

Follow me.
> Jesus speaks to the multitude after healing a paralytic, *Mark* 2:14

Are not two sparrows sold for a penny? And not one of them will fall to the ground without your Father's will. But even the hairs of your head are all numbered. Fear not, therefore; you are of more value than many sparrows.
> Jesus speaks to his disciples of the value of God's human creation, *Matthew* 10:29-31

Oh faithless generation, how long am I to be with you? How long am I to bear with you?
> Jesus speaks to the father of a child with a seizure disorder, *Mark* 9:19

Do you believe in the Son of God? ...You have seen him, and it is he who speaks to you.
> Jesus speaking to those who questioned his identity, *John* 9:35-37

This is the work of God that you believe in him whom he has sent.
> Jesus urges his followers to have faith in the truth of his teaching, *John* 6:29

Daughter, your faith has made you well; go in peace and be healed.
> To a woman Jesus healed from a bleeding disorder, *Mark* 5:34

All things are possible to one who believes.
> *Mark* 9:23

For truly I say to you, if you have faith as a grain of mustard seed, you will say to this mountain, "Move from here to there," and it will move; and nothing will be impossible to you.

The power of belief in healing, *Matthew* 17:20-21

Truly I say to you, if you have faith and never doubt...even if you say to this mountain, "Be taken up and cast into the sea," it will be done. And whatever you ask in prayer you will receive, if you have faith.

On the same theme, *Matthew* 21:21-22

Heaven's kingdom is like a mustard seed, the smallest of all seeds, but when it falls on prepared soil, it produces a large plant and becomes a shelter for birds of the sky.

Thomas 20

When you make the two into one, you will become children of Adam, and when you say, "Mountain, move from here!" it will move.

Thomas 10

Have I been with you so long, and yet you do not know me, Philip? Those who have seen me have seen the Father; how can you say, "Show us the Father"? Do you not believe that I am in the Father and the Father in me? The words that I say to you I do not speak on my own authority; but the Father who dwells in me does his works. Believe me that I am in the Father and the Father is in me; or else believe me for the sake of the works themselves.

To Philip at the Last Supper, *John* 14:9-11

Put your finger here, and see my hands; and put out your hand and place it in my side; do not be faithless, but believing. Have you believed because you have seen me? Blessed are those who have not seen and yet believe.

Jesus speaks to Thomas after the crucifixion, *John* 20:27-29

Truly, truly I say to you when you were young you girded yourself and walked where you would; but when you are old, you will stretch out your hands and another will guide you and carry you where you do not wish to go. Follow me.

To Peter regarding his future (Peter was martyred at Rome A.D. 64), *John* 21:18-19

Why does this generation seek a sign? Truly I say to you, no sign shall be given to this generation.

Mark 8:12

Unless you see signs and wonders you will not believe.

John 4:48

Why are you afraid? Have you no faith?

Mark 4:40

Let not your hearts be troubled; believe in God, believe also in me. In my Father's house there are many rooms. If it were not so, would I have told you that I go to prepare a place for you? And when I go and prepare a place for you, I will come again and will take you to myself that where I am you may be also. And you know the way where I am going.

The promise, *John* 14:1-4

Whoever drinks from my mouth will become like me; I myself shall become that person, and the mysteries will be revealed to him.

Thomas 108

Peace be with you...
John 20

10. PEACE

Peace I leave with you; my peace I give to you; not as the world gives do I give to you. Let not your hearts be troubled, neither let them be afraid.
John 14:27

Come away by yourselves to a solitary place and rest awhile.
Mark 6:31

Come to me all who labor and are heavy laden and I will give you rest. Take my yoke upon you and learn from me, for I am gentle and lowly in heart, and you will find rest unto your souls: For my yoke is easy and my burden is light.
Matthew 11:28-30, *Thomas* 90

Would that even today you knew the things that make for peace! But now they are hid from your eyes.
Luke 19:42

Your faith has made you well. Go in peace.
To a sinful woman who washes his feet with her tears, *Luke* 7:50

And when you go into a household, greet it. If the household is worthy, let your peace come upon it. But if it is not worthy, your peace will return to you.
Matthew 10:12-13, *Luke* 10:5-6

When the Blessed One had said this, he greeted them all saying, "Peace be with you. Receive my peace unto yourselves."
Mary Magdalene, 4:33

Blessed are the peacemakers: for they shall be called the children of God.
Matthew 5:9

Do not lay for yourselves treasures on earth…
Matthew 6:19

11. MONEY

Do not lay up for yourselves treasures on earth where moth and rust consume and where thieves break in and steal, but lay up for yourselves treasures in heaven where neither moth nor rust consumes and where thieves do not break in and steal. For where your treasure is, there will your heart be also.

> Speaking to the multitudes against valuing only the material,
> *Matthew* 6:19-21

Show me a denarius. Whose image and inscription does it have? Render therefore to Caesar the things that are Caesar's, and to God the things that are God's.

> Responding to the Pharisees, chief priests, and scribes who questioned him about paying taxes to Rome,
> *Luke* 20:24-25*, Mark* 12:15-17

Jesus said to the Pharisees, "Show me the tax money. Whose image and inscription is this [upon it]? They responded "Caesar's." And Jesus said, "Render therefore to Caesar the things that are Caesar's, and to God the things that are God's."

> *Matthew* 22:19-21

If you have money, do not lend it at interest. Rather, give [it] to someone from whom you will not get it back.

> *Thomas* 95

Whoever has found the world and has become wealthy, let him renounce the world.

> *Thomas* 110

It is written, "My house shall be called a house of prayer, but you make it a den of robbers."

> Jesus drives the money-changers out of the Temple,
> *Matthew* 21:13

Take these things away. Do not make My Father's house a house of merchandise.

On the same theme, *John* 2:16

Is it not written, "My house shall be called a house of prayer for all nations?" But you have made it a den of thieves.

Mark 11:17

Provide neither gold nor silver nor copper in you money belts, nor bag for your journey, nor two tunics, nor sandals, nor staffs; for a worker is worthy of his food.

Jesus sends his disciples into the world.

Matthew 10:9-10

Children, how hard it is for those who trust in riches to enter the kingdom of God! It is easier for a camel to go through the eye of a needle than for a rich man to enter the kingdom of God.

Mark 10:24-25

There was a rich man who had a great deal of money. He said, "I shall invest my money so that I may sow, reap, plant, and fill my storehouses with produce, that I may lack nothing." These were the things he was thinking in his heart, but that very night he died. Whoever has ears to hear, let them hear!

Thomas 63

The land of a rich man brought forth plentifully; and he thought to himself, "What shall I do, for I have nowhere to store my crops?" And he said, "I will do this: I will pull down my barns, and build larger ones; and there I will store all my grain and my goods. And I will say to my soul, 'Soul, you have ample goods laid up for many years; take your ease, eat, drink, be merry.'" But God said to him "Fool! This night your soul is required of you and the things you have prepared, whose will they be?"

So it will be with he who lays up treasure for himself and is not rich toward God.

Luke 12:16-21

No man can serve two masters, for he will either hate one and love the other, or he will love one and hate the other. You cannot serve God and money.

Matthew 6:24

Provide neither gold nor silver nor copper in your money belts. Nor bag for your money nor two tunics nor sandals nor staffs, for a worker is worthy of his food.

Matthew 10:9

...each will return to its primal source...
Philip

12. THE KINGDOM

[Come], that I may teach you about [secrets] no person [has] ever seen. For there exists a great and boundless realm, whose extent no generation of angels has seen, [in which] there is [a] great invisible [Spirit], which no eye of an angel has ever seen, no thought of the heart has ever comprehended, and it was never called by name.

Judas 3

All nature, all formations, all creatures exist in and with one another, and they will be resolved again into their own roots. For the nature of matter is resolved into the roots of its own nature alone.

Mary Magdalene 4:22-23

It will not come by watching for it. It will not be said, "Look, here!" or "Look, there!" Rather, the Father's kingdom is spread out upon the earth, and people don't see it.

Thomas 113

The kingdom of God is as if a man should scatter seed upon the ground, and should sleep and rise night and day, and the seed should sprout and grow, he himself knows not how. For the earth produces of itself, first the blade, then the head, then the full grain in the head. But when the grain is ripe, at once he puts in the sickle, because the harvest has come.

Jesus speaks to the twelve in parable of planting goodness and having faith, *Mark* 4:26-29

The Kingdom of the Father is like a merchant who had a supply of merchandise and then found a pearl. That merchant was prudent; he sold the merchandise and bought the single pearl for himself.

Thomas 76

59

With what can we compare the kingdom of God, or what parable shall we use for it? It is like a grain of mustard seed, which, when sown upon the ground, is the smallest of all the seeds on earth; yet when it is gown it grows up and becomes the greatest of all shrubs, and puts forth large branches, so that the birds of the air can make nests in its shade.

Mark 4:30-32

Again, the kingdom of heaven is like a merchant in search of fine pearls, who on finding one pearl of great value, went and sold all that he had and bought it.

Matthew 13:45-46

Truly I say to you, today you will be with me in Paradise.

The promise to a criminal crucified with him who repented in the last moment of life, *Luke* 23:43

Truly, truly, I say to you, you will see heaven opened and the angels of the Creator ascending and descending upon the Son of man.

John 1:51

It is possible for you to reach it, but you will grieve a great deal…

Jesus speaks privately to Judas about the kingdom, *Judas* 1

When the Son of Man comes in his glory and all the angels with him, then he will sit on his glorious throne. Before him will be gathered all the nations and he will separate them one from another as a shepherd separates the sheep from the goats and he will place the sheep at his right and but the goats at the left. Then the King will say to those at his right hand, "Come, oh blessed of my Father, inherit the kingdom prepared for you from the foundation of the world."

Matthew 25:31-34

The kingdom of God is like a man who had a treasure hidden in his field but did not know it. And [when] he died, he left it to his [son]. The son [did] not know [about it either]. He took over the field and sold it. The buyer went plowing, [discovered] the treasure, and began to lend money at interest to whomever he wished.

Thomas 109

In my Father's house there are many rooms; if it were not so, I would have told you. I go to prepare a place for you. And if I go and prepare a place for you, I will come again and receive you to myself; that where I am there you may be also.

Jesus responds to Peter at the last supper when Peter asks why he can't follow Jesus .*John* 14:2-3

The star that leads the way is your star.

Judas

If you do not fast from the world, you will not find the kingdom.

Thomas 27

Blessed are those who are solitary and chosen, for you will find the kingdom: for you have come from it, and you will return there again.

Thomas 49

When you make the two into one, and when you make the inner like the outer and the outer like the inner, and the upper like the lower, and when you make male and female into a single one, so that the male will not be male nor the female be female...then you will enter the kingdom. These nursing babies are like those who enter the kingdom.

Thomas 22

The kingdom of God is like leaven, which a woman took and hid in three measures of meal, till the whole was leavened.

Luke 13:20-21

The Kingdom of God is within you.

Luke 17:21

The fields are already ripe for the harvest.
John 4:35

13. NOW

The harvest is plentiful but the laborers are few; pray therefore thc Lord of the harvest to send out laborers into his harvest.

Jesus speaks to his disciples of the multitudes without direction,
Matthew 9:37-38

The harvest is great but the workers are few, so ask the master of the harvest to send workers to the fields.

Thomas 73

The time is fulfilled and the kingdom of God is at hand. Repent and believe in the truth of these words.

After John the Baptist is put in prison Jesus begins to preach,
Mark 1:15

Repent, for the kingdom of heaven is at hand.

When Jesus heard that John had been put in prison,
Matthew 4:17

When the crop ripened, he came quickly carrying a sickle and harvested it. Anyone here with two good ears had better listen!

Thomas 24

Truly I say to you, whatever you bind on earth shall be bound in heaven and whatever you loose on earth shall be loosed in heaven.

Jesus speaks to his followers of the importance of action in life,
*Matthew*18:18

Look at the fig tree and all the trees, as soon as they come out in leaf you see for yourselves and know that the summer is already near. So also, when you see these things taking place, you know that the kingdom of God is near.

Luke 21:29-31

They said to him, "Tell us who you are so that we may believe in you." Jesus said to them, "You search the face of heaven and earth, but you have not come to know the one who stands before you, and you do not know how to understand the present moment."
Thomas 91

His disciples said to him, "When will the rest for the dead take place, and when will the new world come?"
Jesus said to them, "What you look forward to
has already come, but you do not recognize it."
Thomas 51

There was a rich man who had a great deal of money. He said, "I shall invest my money so that I may sow, reap, plant, and fill my storehouses with produce, that I may lack nothing." These were the things he was thinking in his heart, but that very night he died. Whoever has ears to hear, let them hear!
Thomas 63

Farming in the world requires the cooperation of four essential elements. A harvest is gathered into the barn only as a result of the natural action of water, earth, wind, and light. God's farming likewise has four elements: faith, hope, love, and knowledge. Faith is our earth, that in which we take root. Hope is the water through which we are nourished. Love is the wind through which we grow. Knowledge, then, is the light through which we ripen.
Philip

My food is to do the will of the Creator who sent me…to complete that work. Don't you say, "There are yet four months, then comes the harvest?" I tell you, lift up your eyes, and see how the fields are already white for harvest.
John 4:34-35

Follow me.
John 1:43

For many are called, but few are chosen.
Jesus speaks to the chief priests and Pharisees, *Matthew* 22:14

Follow me, and I will make you fishers of men.
Mark 1:17, *Matthew* 4:19

Truth, which existed since the beginning, is sown everywhere and many see it being sown, but few are they who see it being reaped.
Philip

...who reaps receives wages, and gathers fruit for eternal life, so that sower and reaper may rejoice together. For here the saying holds true, "One sows and another reaps." I have sent you to reap that for which you did not labor. Others have labored, and you have entered into their labor.
Jesus speaks to his disciples of the food of life, *John* 4-36:38

When it is evening you say, "It will be fair weather, for the sky is red."...you know how to interpret the appearance of the sky, but you cannot interpret the signs of the times.
Matthew 16:2-3, *Luke* 12:54-56

The kingdom of God is as if man should cast seed into the ground; and should sleep, and rise night and day, and the seed should spring and grow up, he knows not how. For the earth brings forth fruit of herself; first the blade, then the ear, and after that the full corn in the ear. But when the fruit is brought forth, immediately he puts in the sickle, because the harvest is come.
Mark 4:26-29

No one, having put his hand to the plough, and looking back is fit for the kingdom of God.
Luke 9:62

I came to call the lost, the weary, the lonely.
Mark 2:17

14. CHRIST'S PURPOSE

Whoever believes in me believes not in me but in the Father who sent me. And who sees me sees the Father from which I come. I have come as light into the world that whoever believes in me may not remain in darkness. If any one hears my sayings and does not keep them—I do not judge them: For I did not come to judge the world but to save the world. Whoever rejects me and does not receive my sayings has a judge; the word that I have spoken will be their judge on the last day. For I have not spoken on my own authority. The Father who sent me has given me commandment what to say and what to speak. And I know that this commandment is eternal life. What I say, therefore, I say as it has been given to me.

> *John* 12:44-50

Foxes have holes, and birds of the air have nests; but the Son of man has nowhere to lay his head.

> Jesus explains the extent of commitment to those who wanted to follow him, *Luke* 9:58

[Foxes have] their dens and birds have their nests, but the son of man has no place to lie down and rest.

> *Thomas* 86

If I do not wash you, you have no part of me.

> Peter protests as Jesus symbolically washes his feet, *John* 13:8

All authority in heaven and on earth has been given to me. Go therefore and make disciples of all nations, baptizing them in the name of the Father and of the Son and of the Holy Spirit, teaching them to observe all that I have commanded you...
I am with you always to the close of the age.

> *Matthew* 28:18-20

Do you think that I have come to give peace on earth? No, I tell you, but rather division, for from now on in one house there will be five divided: three against two and two against three. They will be divided father against son and son against father, mother against daughter and daughter against her mother, mother-in-law against her daughter-in-law and daughter-in-law against her mother-in-law.

Jesus speaks to the multitudes after being cross examined by the Pharisees, *Luke* 12:51-53

Do not think that I have come to abolish the law and the prophets. I have come not to abolish them but to fulfill them. For truly I say to you, until heaven and earth pass away, not an iota, not a dot will pass from the law until all is accomplished. Whoever then relaxes one of the least of these commandments and teaches men to do so shall be called least in the kingdom of heaven, but whoever does them and teaches them shall be called great in the kingdom of heaven.

From the Sermon on the Mount, *Matthew* 5:17-19

Those who are well have no need of a physician, but those who are sick. I came, not to call the righteous, but the lost, the weary, the lonely.

Jesus responds to the scribes and Pharisees who criticize him for his associations, *Mark* 2:17

Let us go on to the next towns so that I may preach there also, for that is why I came out.

Mark 1:38

...for the Son of Man came to seek and to save the lost.

Luke 19:10

...the Son of Man came eating and drinking, and they say, "Look, a glutton and a drunkard, and friend of tax collectors, and sinners!" Yet wisdom is justified by her children.
Jesus is criticized for associating with those in need,
Matthew 11:19

Have you come out as against a robber, with swords and clubs to capture me? Day after day I was with you in the temple teaching, and you did not seize me. But let the scriptures be fulfilled.
Responding to his arrest under the cloak of darkness,
Mark 14:48-49

I came to cast fire upon the earth and would that it were already kindled! I have a baptism to be baptized with and how I am constrained until it is accomplished!
Mark 10:45

I have cast fire upon the world, and look, I am guarding it until it blazes.
Thomas 10

I have food to eat of which you do not know. My food is to do the will of the Father who sent me and to accomplish His work.
John 4:32-34

Behold, we are going up to Jerusalem and the Son of Man will be delivered to the chief priests and the scribes, and they will condemn Him to death, and deliver Him to the Gentiles, and they will mock Him, and spit on Him, and scourge Him and kill Him, and after three days He will rise.
Jesus speaks to his disciples predicting his fate,
Mark 10:33-34

Have you come out as against a robber, with swords and clubs to capture me? Day after day I sat in the temple

teaching, and you did not seize me. But all this has taken place that the scriptures of the prophets might be fulfilled.
Jesus is arrested at night, against the law, Matthew 26:55-56

Now is my soul troubled. And what shall I say? "Father, save me from this hour?" No, for this purpose I have come to this hour. Father, glorify your name.
John 12:27-28

The Son of humanity must suffer many things and be rejected by the elders and chief priests and scribes, be killed, and on the third day be raised.
Luke 9:22

Oh foolish men, and slow of heart to believe all that the prophets have spoken! Was it not necessary that the Christ should suffer these things and enter into his glory?
After his crucifixion Jesus explains the reason to two disciples on a country road, Luke 24:25-26

I am the good shepherd. I know my own and my own know me, as the Father knows me and I know the Father; and I lay down my life for the sheep. And I have other sheep that are not of this fold; I must bring them also and they will heed my voice. So there shall be one flock, one shepherd.
John 10:14-16

My sheep hear my voice and I know them and they follow me. I give them eternal life, and they shall never perish, and no one shall snatch them out of my hand. My Father, who has given them to me, is greater than all and no one is able to snatch them out of the Father's hand.
John 10:27-29

I must preach the good news of the kingdom of God to the other cities also, for I was sent for this purpose.
Luke 4:43

...Father, the hour has come; glorify your Son that the Son may glorify You since you have given him power over all flesh to give eternal life to all who You have given him. And this is eternal life that they know You the only true God and Jesus Christ who You have sent. I glorified You on earth having accomplished the work which You gave me to do and now, Father, glorify me in Your own presence with the glory which I had with you before the world was made. I have manifested Your name to the men and women who You gave me out of the world. They were Yours and you gave them to me and they have kept Your word. Now they know that everything that You have given me is from you, for I have given them the words which You gave me and they have received them and know in truth that I came from You and they have believed that You sent me. I am praying for them. I am not praying for the world but for those who You gave me for they are Yours. All mine are Yours and all that is Yours are mine and I am glorified in all. And now I am no longer in the world, but they are in the world and I am coming to You. Holy Father, keep them in Your name which You have given to me, that they may be one even as we are one. While I was with them I kept them in Your name, which You have given me. I have guarded them and none of them is lost but the son of perdition, that the scripture might be fulfilled. But now I am coming to You and these things I speak in the world that they may have my joy fulfilled in themselves. I have given them Your word and the world has hated them because they are not of the world, even as I am not of the world. I do not pray that You should take them out of the world, but that You should keep them from the evil one. They are not of the world, even as I am not of the world. Sanctify them in the truth. Your word is truth. As You sent me into the world, so have I sent them into the world; and for their sake I consecrate myself that they also may be consecrated in truth. I do not pray for these only, but also for those who believe in me through their word that they may all be one. Even as you,

Father are in me and I in You, that they also may be is us, so that the world may believe that you have sent me. The glory which You gave me I have given to them that they may be one even as we are one—I in them and You in me, that they may become perfectly one. Then the world may know that You sent me and loved them even as You loved me. Father, I desire that they also may be with me where I am to behold my glory, which You have given me in Your love for me before the foundation of the world. Oh righteous Father, the world has not known You but I have known You and these know that You have sent me. I made known to them Your name and I will make it known that the love with which You have loved me may be in them, and I in them.

> At the last supper, *John* 17:1-26

Truly, truly I say to you, I am the door of the sheep. All who came before me are thieves and robbers; but the sheep did not heed them. I am the door. Who enters by me will be saved, and will go in and out and find pasture. The thief comes only to steal and kill and destroy; I came that they may have life and have it abundantly. I am the good shepherd. The good shepherd lays down his life for his sheep. He who is a hireling and not a shepherd, whose own the sheep are not, sees the wolf coming and leaves the sheep and flees; and the wolf snatches them and scatters them. He flees because he is a hireling and cares nothing for the sheep.

> Responding to the Pharisees who ask, "Are we blind also?"
> *John* 10:7-13

I am the way, and the truth, and the life; no one comes to the Father but by me. If you had known me you would have known my Father also. From now on you know Him and have seen Him.

> At the Passover Supper when Philip asks Jesus to show them the Source of life, *John* 14:6-7

Put your sword into its sheath; shall I not drink the cup the Father has given me?

> To Peter in the garden of Gesthemane; Jesus' acceptance of his destiny, *John* 18:11

Woman, why are you weeping? Whom do you seek? …Mary…do not hold me, for I have not yet ascended to the Father; but go to my brethren and say to them that I am ascending to my Father and your Father, to my God and your God.

> Jesus speaks to Mary Magdalene three days after the crucifixion, *John* 20:15-17

For the Son of man also came not to be served but to serve and to give his life as a ransom for many.

> *Mark* 10:45

It is fulfilled.

> On the cross, his life purpose has been accomplished, *John* 19:3

My Father is working still, and I am working.

> *John* 5:17

Nation will rise against nation, and kingdom against kingdom…
Luke 21:10

15. WAR & CRISIS

Do you see these great buildings? There will not be left here one stone upon another that will not be thrown down.

To his followers who admired the temple, *Mark* 13:2

And when you hear of wars and tumults do not be terrified, for this must first take place, but the end will not be at once. Nation will rise against nation and kingdom against kingdom; there will be great earthquakes and in various places famines and pestilence; and there will be terrors and great signs from heaven.

Jesus responds to those who ask when the temple will be destroyed, *Luke* 21:9-11

And when you hear of wars and rumors of wars do not be alarmed, this must take place, but the end is not yet. For nation will rise against nation, and kingdom against kingdom; there will be earthquakes in various places, there will be famines; this is but the beginning of the sufferings. But take heed to yourselves for they will deliver you up to councils; and you will be beaten in synagogues; and you will stand before governors and kings for my sake, to bear testimony before them. The gospel must first be preached to all nations. And when they bring you to trial and deliver you up, do not be anxious beforehand what you are to say; but say whatever is given you in that hour, for it is not you who speak, but the Spirit of Truth. And brother will deliver up brother to death, and the father his child, and children will rise against parents and have them put to death; and you will be hated by all for my name's sake. But he who endures to the end will be saved. But when you see the desolating sacrilege set up where it ought not to be, then let those who are in Judea flee to the mountains. Let those who are on the housetop not go down, not enter their house to take anything away; and let those who are in the field not turn back to take their coat. Alas for those who are with child and for those who give

75

suck in those days! Pray that it may not happen in winter. For in those days there will be such tribulation as has not been from the beginning of the creation which God created until now and never will be. If the Lord had not shortened the days, no human being would be saved; but for the sake of the elect, whom he chose, he shortened the days. If any one says to you, "Look, here is the Christ!" or "Look, there he is!" do not believe it. False Christs and false prophets will arise and show signs and wonders to lead astray, if possible, the elect. But take heed; I have told you all things beforehand.

But in those days, after that tribulation, the sun will be darkened, and the moon will not give its light and the stars will be falling from heaven and the powers in the heavens will be shaken. And then they will see the Son of man coming in clouds with great power and glory. And then he will send out the angels, and gather his elect from the four winds, from the ends of the earth to the ends of heaven.

Mark 13:5-27

Perhaps people think that I have come to cast peace upon the world. They do not know that I have come to cast conflicts upon the earth—fire, sword, and war. For there will be five in a house: there will be three against two and two against three, father against son and son against father, and they will stand alone.

Thomas 16

Do you think that I have come to give peace on earth? No, I tell you, but rather division; for from now on in one house there will be five divided: three against two and two against three. They will be divided father against son and son against father, mother against daughter and daughter against her mother, mother-in-law against her daughter-in-law and daughter-in-law against her mother-in-law.

Luke 12:51-53

Do not think that I have come to bring peace on earth; I have not come to bring peace, but a sword. For I have come to set a man against his father and a daughter against her mother and a daughter-in-law against her mother-in-law; and a man's foes will be those of his own household.

The choice between spirit and blood, *Matthew* 10:34-36

But of that day or that hour no one know, not even the angels in heaven, nor the Son of Man, but only the Creator. Take heed, watch and pray; for you do not know when the time will come. It is like one going on a journey, when he leaves home and puts the servants in charge, each with his work, and commands the doorkeeper to be on the watch. Watch therefore for you do not know when the owner of the house will come, in the evening or at midnight, or at cockcrow, or in the morning, lest he come suddenly and find you asleep. And what I say to you I say to all: Watch.

Mark 13:32-37

Truly, truly I say to you, you will see heaven opened and the angels of the Father ascending and descending upon the Son of Man.

Jesus speaks to Nathaniel who questioned, "Can anything good come out of Nazareth?" *John* 1:51

And there will be signs in sun and moon and stars, and upon the earth distress of nations in perplexity at the roaring of the sea and the waves. Men and women fainting with fear and with foreboding of what is coming on the world; for the powers of the heavens will be shaken. And then they see the Son of man coming in a cloud with power and great glory. Now when these things begin to take place look up and raise your heads, because your redemption is drawing near.

Luke 21:25-28

Daughters of Jerusalem do not weep for me but weep for yourselves and for your children. For behold the days are coming when they will say, "Blessed are the barren and the

wombs that never bore and the breasts that never gave suck!"
Then they will begin to say to the mountains, "Fall on us,"
and to the hills, "Cover us." For if they do this when the
wood is green, what will happen when it is dry?

A warning. Jerusalem was destroyed in A.D. 70,
Luke 23:28:31

Watch therefore, for you know neither the day nor the hour.

Matthew 25:13

You will be delivered up even by parents and brothers and
kinsmen and friends and some of you they will put to death;
you will be hated by all for my name's sake. But not a hair of
your head will perish.

Luke 21:16-18

Behold, I send you out as sheep in the midst of wolves, so be
wise as serpents and innocent as doves. Beware of men for
they will deliver you up to councils, and flog you in their
synagogues, and you will be dragged before governors and
kings for my sake, to bear testimony before them and the
Gentiles. When they deliver you up, do not be anxious how
you are to speak or what you are to say; for what you are to
say will be given to you in that hour; for it is not you who
speak, but the Spirit of Truth speaking through you. Brother
will deliver up brother to death, and the father his child and
children will rise against parents and have them put to death,
and you will be hated by all for my namesake. But whoever
endures to the end will be saved.

Jesus instructs the newly chosen disciples about loyalty to the
true path in time of crisis, *Matthew* 10:16-22

78

O Jerusalem, Jerusalem, killing the prophets and stoning those who are sent to you! How often would I have gathered your children together as a hen gathers her brood under wings, and you would not!

Jesus speaks to the Pharisees, *Luke* 13:34

Then they will deliver you up to tribulation and put you to death, and you will be hated by all nations for my name's sake. And then many will fall away and betray one another and hate one another. And many false prophets will arise and lead many astray. And because wickedness is multiplied, love will grow cold. But he who endures to the end will be saved.

Matthew 24:9-13

All who live by the sword will perish by the sword.

To Peter in the garden of Gesthemane when he cut off the Roman soldier's ear, *Matthew* 26:52

And do not fear those who kill the body but cannot kill the soul. But rather fear Him who is able to destroy both soul and body in hell.

Matthew 10:28, *Luke* 12:4-5

Every kingdom divided against itself is brought to desolation; and every city or house divided against itself shall not stand: and if Satan cast out Satan, he is divided against himself; how shall his kingdom stand? And if I by Beelzebub cast out devils, by whom do your children cast them out? Therefore they shall be your judges. But if I cast out devils by the Spirit of God, then the kingdom of God is come unto you. Or else how can one enter into a strong man's house and spoil his goods, except he first bind the strong man, and then he will spoil his house.

Jesus responds to the Pharisees who accuse him of casting out devils in the name of Satan, *Matthew* 12:25-29

Blessed are the eyes that see what you see!
Luke 10:23

16. AWAKENED PERCEPTION

One perceives through neither soul nor spirit but by mind, which mediates between both; visions are mental.
> Jesus responds to Mary Magdalene, *Mary Magdalene*

Blessed are the eyes that see what you see! For I tell you that many prophets and kings desired to see what you see and did not see it, and to hear what you hear, and did not hear it.
> Speaking to his disciples of their vision in the perception of truth, *Luke* 10:23-24

I took my stand in the midst of the world, and in flesh I appeared to them. I found them all drunk, and I did not find any of them thirsty. My soul ached for the children of humanity, because they are blind in their hearts and do not see, for they came into the world empty, and they also seek to depart from the world empty.
> *Thomas* 28

Listen! A sower went out to sow. And as he sowed, some seed fell along the path, and the birds came and devoured it. Other seed fell on rocky ground where it had not much soil, and immediately it sprang up, since it had no depth of soil; and when the sun rose it was scorched, and since it had no root it withered away. Other seed fell among thorns and the thorns grew up and choked it, and it yielded no grain. And other seeds fell into good soil and brought forth grain, growing up and increasing and yielding thirtyfold and sixtyfold and a hundredfold. ...Those who have ears to hear, let them hear.
> Teaching in parables from the boat to those on shore on the depth of human of intention, *Mark* 4:3-9

Look, the sower went out, took a handful [of seeds], and scattered them. Some fell on the road, and the birds came and gathered them. Others fell on rock, and they did not take root in the soil or produce any heads of grain. Others fell among the thorns, and the thorns choked the seeds and worms consumed them. Still others fell on good soil, and it brought forth a good crop: it yielded sixty per measure and one hundred twenty per measure.

Thomas 9

It is impossible [44] to sow seed on [rock] and harvest its fruit.

In reference to hardness of heart, *Judas*

Let them alone; they are blind guides. And if a blind man leads a blind man, both will fall into a pit.

Concerning religious men who opposed Jesus, *Matthew* 15:14

If a blind person leads a blind person, both of them will fall into a hole.

Thomas 34

But to what shall I compare this generation? It is like children sitting in the market places and calling to their playmates, "We piped to you and you did not dance; we wailed, and you did not mourn."

Speaking to the people about John the Baptist and the perception of truth versus the perceptions of the masses, *Matthew* 11:16-17

Blessed are you, Simon Bar-Jona! For flesh and blood has not revealed this to you but my Father who is in heaven. And I tell you, you are Peter, and on this rock I will build my temple, and the powers of death shall not prevail against it. I will give you the keys of the kingdom of heaven, and whatever you bind on earth shall be bound in heaven and whatever you loose on earth shall be loosed in heaven.

Jesus speaks of Simon's strength of character as representative of a true follower, *Matthew* 16:17-19

When you see a cloud rising in the west, you say at once, "A shower is coming," and so it happens. And when you see the south wind blowing, you say, "There will be scorching heat," and it happens. You hypocrites! You know how to interpret the appearance of earth and sky; but why do you not know how to interpret the present time?

Luke 12:54-56

When it is evening you say, "It will be fair weather, for the sky is red." And in the morning, "It will be stormy today, for the sky is red and threatening." You know how to interpret the appearance of the sky, but you cannot interpret the signs of the times.

On the same theme, *Matthew* 16:2-3

Let your loins be girded and your lamps burning, and be like those who are waiting for their master to come home from the marriage feast, so that they may open to him at once when he comes and knocks. Blessed are those servants whom the master finds awake when he comes; truly I say to you, he will gird himself and have them sit at table, and he will come and serve them. If he comes in the second watch, or in the third and finds them awake, blessed are those servants! But know this, that if the householder had known at what hour the thief was coming, he would have been awake and would not have left his house to be broken into. You also must be ready; for the Son of man is coming at an hour you do not expect.

Jesus speaks to his disciples of full presence in every moment, *Luke* 12:35-40

Are your hearts hardened? Having eyes do you not see, and having ears do you not hear?

To his followers when they failed to understand, *Mark* 8:17-18

A nobleman went into a far country to receive kingly power and then return. Calling ten of his servants, he gave them ten coins and said to them, "Trade with these until I come." But his citizens hated him and sent an embassy after him saying, "We do not want this man to reign over us." When he returned, having received the kingly power, he commended these servants to whom he had given the money to be called to him that he might know what they had gained by trading. The first came before him saying, "Lord, your coin has made ten more." And he said to him, "Well done good servant! Because you have been faithful in very little, you shall have authority over ten cities." And the second came saying, "Lord, your coin has made five coins." And he said to him, "And you are to have authority over five cities." Then another came saying, "Lord, here is your coin, which I kept laid away in a napkin; for I was afraid of you because you are a severe man. You take up what you did not lay down and reap what you did not sew." And the lord of the land said to him, "I will condemn you out of your own mouth, you wicked servant! You knew that I was a severe man, taking up what I did not lay down and reaping what I did not sow! Why then did you not put my money into the bank and at my coming I should have collected it with interest?" And he said to those who stood by, "Take the coin from him and give it to him who has the ten coins." And they said to him, "Lord, he already has ten coins!" "I tell you that to every one who has will more be given; but from him who has not, even what he has will be taken away."

A parable on the use of God's gifts, *Luke* 19:12-26

Those who have something in hand will be given more, and those who have nothing will be deprived of even the little they have.

Thomas 41

Truly, truly I say to you, we speak of what we know and bear witness to what we have seen. But you do not receive our testimony. If I have told you earthly things and you do not believe, how can you believe if I tell you heavenly things? No one has ascended into heaven but he who descended from heaven, the Son of man. And as Moses lifted up the serpent in the wilderness, so must the Son of man be lifted up, that whoever believes in him may have eternal life.

Jesus speaks to a Pharisee, *John* 3:11-15

Not all men can receive this precept, but only those to whom it is given. For there are eunuchs who have been so from birth and there are eunuchs who have been made eunuchs by men and there are eunuchs who have made themselves eunuchs for the sake of the kingdom of heaven. He who is able to receive this, let him receive it.

Eunuch here means one who is celibate, *Matthew* 19:11-12

My teaching is not mine but of the Father who sent me. If anyone's will is to do the will of the Father, he shall know whether the teaching is from God or whether I am speaking on my own authority. He who speaks on his own authority seeks his own glory, but he who seeks the glory of the Father is true. In him there is no falsehood.

Jesus speaks to the Jews in the temple of awareness of the voice of truth, *John* 7:16-18

I shall give you what no eye has seen, what no ear has heard, what no hand has touched, what has never arisen in a human heard.

Thomas 27

Watch therefore for you do not know when the owner of the house will come, in the evening or at midnight, or at cockcrow, or in the morning—lest he come suddenly and find you asleep. And what I say to you I say to all: Watch.

Mark 13:32-37

I send you forth as sheep in the midst of wolves: be wise as serpents and innocent as doves.

Matthew 10:16

He who hears you hears me; and he that despises you despises me; and he that despises me despises him that sent me.

Luke 10:16

The old man in days will not hesitate to ask a little child seven days old about the place of life, and that person will live.

Thomas 4

17. CHILDREN

Whoever becomes like a child will recognize the kingdom.
Thomas

Whoever receives one such child in my name receives me; and whoever receives me receives not me but who sent me.
Mark 9:37

And whoever gives to one of these little ones even a cup of cold water because he is a disciple, truly I say to you, he shall not lose his reward.
Matthew 10:42

But I have said that whoever among you becomes a child will recognize the [Father's] kingdom and will become greater than John.
Thomas 46

Let the children come, do not hinder them; for to such belongs the kingdom of God. Truly I say to you, whoever does not receive the kingdom of God like a child shall not enter it.
Mark 10:14-15

I thank you, Creator of heaven and earth that you have hidden these things from the wise and understanding and revealed them to babes. Yes, for such was your gracious will. All things have been delivered to me by the Father and no one knows who the Son is except the Father or who the Father is except the Son and any one to whom the Son chooses to reveal him.
Luke 10:21-22

If flesh came into being because of spirit, that is a marvel, but if spirit came into being because of the body, that is a marvel of marvels...

Spiritual rebirth, *Thomas* 29

Whoever causes one of these little ones who believe in me to sin, it would be better for him if a great millstone were hung round his neck and he were thrown into the sea.

Jesus speaks to John of the corruption of the innocent as the greatest crime, *Mark* 9:42

Truly, truly I say to you, unless one is born of water and spirit he cannot enter the kingdom of God. That which is born of the flesh is flesh, and that which is born of the spirit is spirit. Do not marvel that I say to you, "You must be born anew." The wind blows where it wishes and you hear the sound of it, but you do not know where it comes or where it goes. So it is with every one who is born of the spirit.

Speaking of spiritual birth to Nicodemus, a Pharisee and ruler of the Jews, *John* 3:5-8

All things have been delivered to me by my Father: and no one knows the Son except the Father, and no one knows the Father except the Son and any one to whom the Son chooses to reveal Him.

Jesus grows impatient with those who do not receive his word, *Matthew* 11:27

I thank you Creator, Lord of heaven and earth, that you have hidden these things from the wise and understanding and revealed them to babes.

On the same theme, *Matthew* 11:25

Truly I say to you, unless you turn and become like children, you will never enter the kingdom of heaven. Whoever humbles himself like this child is the greatest in the kingdom of heaven.

Whoever receives one such child in my name receives me.

Matthew 18:3-5

See that you do not despise one of these little ones, for I tell you that in heaven their angels always behold the face of my Father who is in heaven.

The beauty of creation in the child, *Matthew* 18:10-11

If anyone becomes a child of the light he will receive the light. If anyone does not receive it while he is here, he will not be able to receive it in the other place.

Philip

A woman when she is in travail has sorrow, because her hour is come: but as soon as she is delivered of the child, she remembers no more the anguish, for joy that a child is born into the world.

John 16:21

Often he did not appear to his disciples as himself, but he was found among them as a child.

Judas

...the measure you give will be the measure you will get.
Matthew: 7:2

18. JUDGMENT

Judge not that you not be judged. For with the judgment you pronounce you will be judged, and the measure you give will be the measure you get. Why do you see the speck that is in your brother's eye, but do not notice the log that is in your own eye? Or how can you say to your brother, "Let me take the speck out of your eye," when there is the log in your own eye? You hypocrite, first take the log out of your own eye, and then you will see clearly to take the speck out of your brother's eye.

From the Sermon on the Mount, *Matthew* 7:1-5

Judge not and you will not be judged. Condemn not and you will not be condemned. Forgive and you will be forgiven. Give and it will be given to you.

Luke 6:37-38

You see the sliver in your friend's eye, but you don't see the timber in your own eye. When you take the timber out of your own eye, then you will see well enough to remove the sliver from your friend's eye.

Thomas 26

I can do nothing on my own authority, as I hear, I judge and my judgment is just, because I seek not my own will but the will of the Father who sent me.

Jesus speaks to the orthodox Jews who accuse Him of healing on the Sabbath, *John* 5:30

For judgment I came into this world, that those who do not see may see and that those who see may become blind.

Jesus speaks to the Pharisees, *John* 9:39

Truly, truly I say to you, the Son can do nothing of His own accord, but only what He sees the Father doing, for whatever

He does, that the Son does likewise. For the Father loves the Son, and shows Him all that He Himself is doing; and greater works than these will He show Him, that you may marvel.
For as the Father raises the dead and gives them life, so also the Son gives life to whomever He will. The Father judges no one, but has given all judgment to the Son, that all may honor the Son, even as they honor the Father. He who does not honor the Son does not honor the Father who sent Him. Truly, truly I say to you, he who hears my word and believes Him who sent me, has eternal life; he does not come into judgment, but has passed from death to life.

> *John 5:19-24*

Now is the judgment of this world. Now shall the ruler of this world be cast out and I, when I am lifted up from the earth, will draw all humankind to myself.

> Jesus prepares for the crucifixion, *John* 12:31-32

The kingdom of heaven is like a householder who went out early in the morning to hire laborers for his vineyard. After agreeing with the laborers for a denarius a day, he sent them into his vineyard. And going out about the third hour he saw others standing idle in the market place and to them he said, "You go into the vineyard too, and whatever is right I will give you." So they went. Going out again about the sixth hour and the ninth hour, he did the same. And about the eleventh hour he went out and found others standing and he said to them, "Why do you stand here idle all day?" They said to him, "Because no one has hired us." He said to them, "You go into the vineyard too." And when evening came, the owner of the vineyard said to his steward, "Call the laborers and pay them their wages, beginning with the last up to the first." And when those hired about the eleventh hour came, each of them received a denarius. Now when the first came they thought they would receive more; but each of them also received a denarius. And on receiving it they grumbled at the householder saying, "These last worked only one hour and you have made them equal to us who have borne the burden of the day and the scorching heat." But he replied to one of the, "Friend, I am doing you no wrong; did you not agree with me for a denarius? Take what belongs to you, and go. I choose to give to this last as I give to you. Am I not allowed to do what I choose with what belongs to me? Or do you begrudge my generosity?"

> Jesus explains to the disciples the need to avoid making comparisons to others. *Matthew* 20:1-15

If you were blind you would have no sin; but now you say, "We see." therefore your sin remains.

> To the Pharisees who claim to have full understanding yet do not act accordingly, *John* 9:41

No good tree bears bad fruit nor again does a bad tree bear good fruit; for each tree is known by its own fruit. Figs are not gathered from thorns, nor are grapes picked from a bramble bush. The good man out of the good treasure of his heart produces good and the evil man out of his evil treasure produces evil. For out of the abundance of the heart his mouth speaks.

> A parable from the Sermon on the Mount, *Luke* 6:43-45

Just as the weeds are gathered and burned with fire, so will it be at the close of the age…

> Jesus explains to his disciples that good will prevail,
> *Matthew* 13:40

Let him who is without sin among you be the first to throw a stone at her...Woman, where are they? Has no one condemned you? ...Neither do I condemn you; go and sin no more.

> To the scribes and Pharisees, who brought a woman caught in adultery before him, Jesus makes it clear that no one is in a position to condemn another, *John* 8:7-11

I did not say these things to you from the beginning because I was with you. But now I am returning to the Father, yet none of you asks me, "Where are you going?" But because I have said these things to you sorrow has filled your hearts. Nevertheless I tell you the truth: it is to your advantage that I go away, for if I do not go away, the Counselor will not come to you; but if I go, I will send the Counselor to you. And when the Counselor comes he will convince the world of sin and of righteousness and of judgment; of sin because they do not believe in me, of righteousness because I go to the Father and you will see me no more; of judgment because the ruler of this world is judged.

> Discourse at the Passover Supper, *John* 16:4-11

The bodily forms will not deceive him, but he will look at the condition of the soul of each one and speak with him. There are many animals in the world which are in a human form. When he identifies them, to the swine he will throw acorns, to the cattle he will throw barley and chaff and grass, to the dogs he will throw bones. To the slaves he will give only the elementary lessons, to the children he will give the complete instruction.

> *Philip*

The kingdom of heaven is like a man who sowed good seed in his field. But while everyone was sleeping, his enemy came and sowed weeds among the wheat and went away. When the wheat sprouted and formed heads, then the weeds also appeared. The owner's servants came to him and said, "Sir, didn't you sow good seed in your field? Where then did the weeds come from?"

He replied, "An enemy did this."

The servants asked him, "Do you want us to go and pull them up?"

"No," he answered, "because while you are pulling the weeds, you may root up the wheat with them. Let them both grow together until the harvest. At that time I will tell the harvesters, 'first collect the weeds and tie them in bundles to be burned, then gather the wheat and bring it into my barn.'"

Matthew 13:24-29

The one who sowed the good seed is the Son of Man. The field is the world, and the good seed stands for the sons of the kingdom. The weeds are the sons of the evil one, and the enemy who sows them is the devil. The harvest is the end of the age, and the harvesters are angels. As the weeds are pulled up and burned in the fire, so it will be at the end of the age. The Son of Man will send out his angels, and they will weed out of his kingdom everything that causes sin and all who do evil. They will throw them into the fiery furnace where there will be weeping and gnashing of teeth. Then the righteous will shine like the sun in the kingdom of their Father. He who has ears, let him hear.

Matthew 13:37-43

I was thirsty and you gave me to drink.
Matthew: 25:35

19. TRUTH IN ACTION

Not everyone who says to me, "Lord, Lord," shall enter the kingdom of heaven, but he who does the will of my Father who is in heaven.

Speaking to the multitudes of the power of actions,
Matthew 7:21

I tell you, if my followers were silent, the very stones would cry out.

Jesus responds to the Pharisees who urge him to silence his followers, *Luke* 19:40

A man had two sons and he went to the first and said, "Son, go and work in the vineyard today." And he answered, "I will not," but afterward he repented and went. And he went to the second and said the same and he answered, "I will go sir," but did not go. Which of the two did the will of his father?

Speaking to the chief priests and elders who question his authority; Jesus gives a comparison of which of them, by their actions, is actually doing the will of God, *Matthew* 21:28-31

Those who come to me and hear my words and do them, I will show what they are like: they are like one building a house, digging deep and laying the foundation upon rock; and when a flood arose, the stream broke against that house, and could not shake it, because it had been well built. But who hears my words and does not do them is like one who builds a house on the ground without a foundation; against which the stream broke and immediately it fell and the ruin of that house was great.

From the Sermon on the Mount Jesus speaks of perseverance deeply rooted in faith and action, *Luke* 6:47-49

Will you also go away?

Jesus speaks to his followers in the Garden of Gesthemane,
John 6:67

For truly I say to you that whoever gives you a cup of water to drink because you bear the name of Christ, will by no means lose their reward.

Mark: 9:41

Every one then who hears these words of mine and does them will be like a wise man who built his house upon the rock, and the rain fell, and the floods came, and the winds blew, and beat upon that house but it did not fall because it has been founded on the rock. And every one who hears these words of mine and does not do them will be like a foolish man who built his house upon the sand, and the rain fell, and the floods came, and the winds blew, and beat against that house, and it fell and great was the fall of it.

Matthew 7:24-27

This is my body, which is given for you. Do this in remembrance of me.

Sharing bread at the Passover Supper, *Luke* 22:19

Every scribe who has been trained for the kingdom of heaven is like a householder who brings out of his treasure what is new and what is old.

Jesus speaks to the disciples of self-renewal, *Matthew* 13:52

Hear me all of you and understand; there is nothing outside of a man which by going into him can defile him, but the things which come out of a man are what defiles him.

Jesus speaks to the multitudes of outward actions after the Pharisees accuse him of eating without washing his hands, *Mark* 7:14-16

...When you go into any country and wander around from place to place, and the people receive you, eat what they serve you and heal the sick among them. For what goes into your mouth will not defile you, rather, it is what comes out of your mouth that will defile you.

Thomas 14

Whoever believes and is baptized will be saved, but whoever does not believe will be condemned. And these signs will accompany those who believe: in my name they will cast out demons, they will speak in new tongues, they will pick up serpents, and if they drink any deadly thing, it will not hurt them. They will lay their hands on the sick and they will recover.

After the resurrection Jesus speaks to his disciples,
Mark 16:16-18

What I tell you in the dark, utter in the light, and what you hear whispered, proclaim upon the housetops.

After the resurrection, *Matthew* 10:27

When they bring you before the synagogues and the rulers and the authorities, do not be anxious how or what you are to answer or what you are to say, for the Holy Spirit will teach you in that very hour what you ought to say.

Jesus speaks to his disciples, *Luke* 12:11_12

What comes out of a man is what defiles a man. For from within, out of the heart of man come evil thoughts, fornication, theft, murder, adultery, coveting, wickedness, deceit. Licentiousness envy, slander, pride, foolishness. All these evil things come from within and they defile a man.

Mark 7:20-23

You are the salt of the earth. But if salt loses its taste…it is good for nothing, but to be cast out, and trodden under foot.

Matthew 5:13

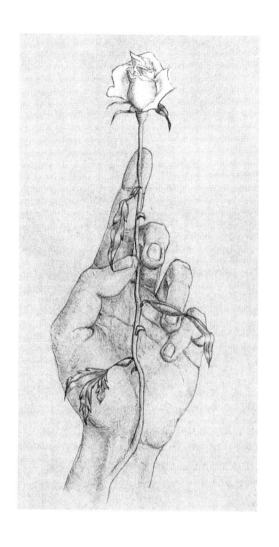

Love one another as I have loved you.
John: 13:34

20. LOVE

Love never controls. It doesn't claim this is "yours" and this is "mine" but says, "All is yours!"
Philip

A new commandment I give you, that you love one another; even as I have loved you, that you also love one another. By this all will know that you are my disciples, if you have love for one another.
At the Passover Supper, *John* 13:34-35

You are my friends if you do what I command you. No longer do I call you servants, for the servant does not know what his master is doing; but I have called you friends, for all that I have heard from my Father I have made known to you. You did not choose me, but I chose you and appointed you that you should go and bear fruit and that your fruit should abide; so that whatever you ask the Father in my name, He may give it to you. This I command you, to love one another.
John 15:14-17

I will not leave you desolate; I will come to you. Yet a little while, and the world will see me no more, but you will see me; because I live, you will live also. In that day you will know that I am one with our Creator, and you in me, and I in you. Those who have my commandments and keep them, they are the ones who love me and whoever loves me will be loved by my Father, and I will love them and manifest myself to them.
Jesus speaks to his disciples before he is crucified,
John 14:18-19

...If a man or woman loves me, they will keep my words, and God will love them, and we will come to them and make our home with them. Whoever does not love me does not keep my words; and the word which you hear is not mine but the Father from which I was sent.

On the same theme, *John* 14:20-21

If anyone loves me, he will keep my word; and my Father will love him, and we will come to him and make our home with him. Those who do not love me do not keep my words; and the word that you hear is not mine but the Father's who sent me.

John 14: 23-24

But I say to you that hear, love your enemies, do good to those who hate you, bless those who curse you, pray for those who abuse you. To him who strikes you on the cheek, offer the other also; and from him who takes away your cloak do not withhold your coat as well. Give to every one who begs from you; and of one who takes away your goods do not ask them again. And as you wish that others would do to you, do so to them. If you love those who love you, what credit is that to you? For even sinners love those who love them. And if you do good to those who do good to you, what credit is that to you? For even wrongdoers do the same. And if you lend to those from whom you hope to receive, what credit is that to you? Even evildoers lend to sinners, to receive as much again. But love your enemies, and do good, and lend, expecting nothing in return; and your reward will be great, and you will be sons and daughters of the Most High; for our Father is kind to the ungrateful and the selfish. Be merciful, even as your Father is merciful.

Luke 6:27-36

You have heard that it was said, "You shall love your neighbor and hate your enemy." But I say to you, love your enemies and pray for those who persecute you, so that you

may be sons of your Father in heaven; for the sun rises on the evil and on the good, and rain falls on the just and on the unjust. For if you love those who love you, what reward have you? Do not even the tax collectors do the same? And if you salute only your friends, what more are you doing that anyone else? Do not even the Gentiles do the same? You, therefore, must be perfect as your Father in heaven is perfect.
From the Sermon on the Mount, *Matthew* 5:43-4

As the Father has loved me, so have I loved you; abide in my love. If you keep my commandments, you will abide in my love, just as I have kept my Father's commandments and abide in that perfect love. These things I have spoken to you, that my joy may be in you, and that your joy may be full.
John 15:9-11

Do you see this woman? I entered your house, you gave me no water for my feet but she has wet my feet with her tears and wiped them with her hair. You gave me no kiss, but from the time I came in she has not ceased to kiss my feet. You did not anoint my head with oil, but she has anointed my feet with ointment. Therefore I tell you, her sins, which are many are forgiven, for she loved much; but he who is forgiven little, loves little.
The devotion of Mary Magdalene, *Luke* 7:44-47

Love your brother like your soul; protect him like the pupil of your eye.
Thomas 25

Faith receives, love gives. No one will be able to receive without faith. No one will be able to give without love…if one gives without love he has no profit from what he has given.
Philip

They honor me with their lips but not with their hearts.
Matthew: 15:8

21. HYPOCRISY & FASLEHOOD

You hypocrites! Well did Isaiah prophesy of you when he said, "This people honors me with their lips, but their heart is far from me; in vain do they worship me, teaching as doctrines the precepts of men."
> Jesus speaks to the chief priests, *Matthew* 15:7-9

It is written, "My house shall be called a house of prayer, but you make it a den of rebbers."
> Jesus drives the money lenders out of the Temple,
> *Matthew* 21:13

Woe to you, scribes and Pharisees, hypocrites! For you are like whitewashed tombs, which outwardly appear beautiful, but within they are full of dead men's bones and all uncleanness. So you also outwardly appear righteous to men, but within you are full of hypocrisy and iniquity.
> Responding to a Pharisee who criticized him for not washing
> before breaking bread, *Luke* 11:42

Beware of the scribes who like to go about in long robes and to have salutations in the market places and the best seats in the synagogues and the places of honor at feasts, who devour widow's houses and for a pretence make long prayers. They will receive the greater condemnation.
> Jesus speaks of religious gestures lacking inner truth,
> *Mark* 12:38-40

You brood of vipers! How can you speak good when you are evil? For out of the abundance of the heart the mouth speaks. The good man out of his good treasure brings forth good and the evil man out of his evil treasure brings forth evil. I tell you on the day of judgment men will render account for every careless word they utter; for by your words you will be justified, and by your words you will be condemned.

To the Pharisees who accuse Jesus of curing the sick in the name of Satan, *Matthew* 12:34-37

Grapes are not harvested from thorn trees, nor are figs gathered from thistles, for they yield no fruit. Good persons produce good from what they have stored up; bad persons produce evil from the wickedness they have stored up in their hearts, and say evil things. For from the overflow of the heart they bring forth evil.

Thomas 45

Truly, I say to you, the tax collectors and the harlots go into the kingdom of God before you.

Speaking to the chief priests and elders of the temple who questioned him, *Matthew* 21:31

You hypocrites! You know how to interpret the appearance of the earth and sky; but why do you not know how to interpret the present time?

Luke 12:56

Well did Isaiah prophesy of you hypocrites, as it is written, "These people honor me with their lips, but their heart is far from me; in vain do they worship me, teaching as doctrines the precepts of men." You leave the commandment of God, and hold fast the tradition of men.

Jesus condemns the Pharisees for their hypocrisy when they fault him and his followers for not washing their hands before eating, *Mark* 7:6-8

Thus, when you give alms, sound no trumpet before you, as the hypocrites do in the synagogues and in the streets, that they may be praised by others. Truly, I say to you, they have their reward. But when you give alms, do not let your left hand know what your right hand is doing, so that your alms may be in secret; and your Father who sees in secret will reward you.

From the Sermon on the Mount, *Matthew* 6:2-4

Beware of practicing your piety before others in order to be seen by them. Then you will have no reward from your Father who is in heaven.

From the Sermon on the Mount on the privacy of prayer, *Matthew* 6:1

Who to you, scribes and Pharisees, hypocrites! For you pay tithe of mint and anise and cumin, and have neglected the weightier matters of the law: justice and mercy and faith. These you ought to have done, without leaving the others undone. Blind guides, who strain out a gnat and swallow a camel!

Speaking to the multitudes and his disciples, *Matthew* 23:23-24

Beware of the leaven of the Pharisees, which is hypocrisy. For there is nothing covered that will not be revealed, nor hidden that will not be known. Therefore whatever you have spoken in the dark will be heard in the light, and what you have spoken in the ear in inner rooms will be proclaimed on the housetops.

Luke 12:2-3

Now you Pharisees make the outside of the cup and dish clean, but your inward part is full of greed and wickedness. Foolish ones! Did not He who made the outside make the inside also?

Jesus' response to the Pharisees on outer appearances versus inner when they criticize him for not washing his hands before eating, *Luke* 11:39-40

Judas, would you betray the Son of Man with a kiss?

Luke 22:48

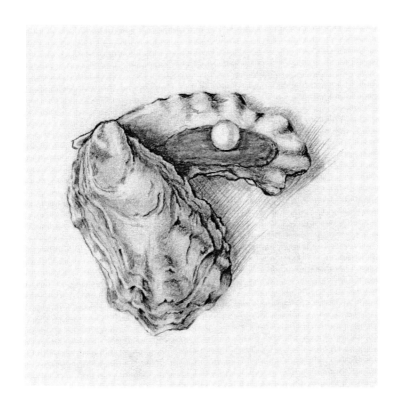

...when he found one pearl of great value...
he went and sold all that he had...
Matthew: 13:46

22. VALUES

The Father's kingdom is like a merchant who had a supply of merchandise and found a pearl. That merchant was prudent; he sold the merchandise and bought the single pearl for himself. So also with you, seek the treasure that is unfailing, that is enduring, where no moth comes to eat and no worm destroys.
Thomas 76

If you would be perfect, go, sell what you possess and give to the poor, and you will have treasure in heaven; and come, follow me. ...Truly, I say to you, it will be hard for a rich man to enter the kingdom of heaven. Again I tell you, it is easier for a camel to go through the eye of a needle than for a rich man to enter the kingdom of God.
Jesus speaks to one who was faithful to the teachings of Moses, but rich in material possessions, *Matthew* 19:21-24

His disciples said to him, "Is circumcision useful or not?"
Jesus said to them, "If it were useful, their father would produce children already circumcised from their mother. Rather, the true circumcision in spirit has become profitable in every respect."
Circumcision as metaphor, *Thomas* 53

Truly, truly I say to you, you seek me, not because you saw signs, but because you ate of the loaves and were filled. Do not labor for the food that perishes, but for the food that endures to eternal life, which the Son of humankind will give to you, for on him has God the Father set his seal.
Jesus speaks about nourishment of the soul, *John* 6:26-27

Gather up the fragments left over, that nothing may be lost.
After distributing the loaves and fish, *John* 6:12

Truly, truly I say to you, it was not Moses who gave you the bread from heaven; my Father gives you the true bread from heaven. For the bread of God is that which comes down from heaven and gives life to the world.

On the same theme, *John* 6:32-33

I am the bread of life; those who come to me shall not hunger, and they who believe in me shall never thirst. But I said to you that you have seen me and yet do not believe. All that the Father gives me will come to me; and they who come to me I will not cast out. For I have come down from heaven, not to do my own will, but the will of the Father who sent me; and this is the will of the Father, that I should lose nothing of all that has been given to me, but raise it up at the last day. For this is the will of God, that every one who sees the Son and believes in him should have eternal life; and I will raise them up at the last day.

Jesus proclaims his teaching as the substance of life,
John 6:35-40

None can come to me unless the Father who sent me draws them; and I will raise them up at the last day. It is written in the prophets, "And they shall all be taught by God." Every one who has heard and learned from the Father comes to me. Not that any one has seen the Father except him who is from God; he has seen the Father. Truly, truly I say to you, who believes has eternal life. I am the bread of life. Your fathers ate the manna in the wilderness and they died. This is the bread, which comes down from heaven, that one may eat of it and not die. I am the living bread, which came down from heaven; if any one eats of this bread, they will live forever; and the bread, which I shall give for the life of the world, is my flesh.

On the same theme, *John* 6:44-51

Truly, truly I say to you, unless you eat the flesh of the Son of Man and drink his blood, you have no life in you; he who eats my flesh and drinks my blood has eternal life, and I will raise him up at the last day. For my flesh is food indeed, and my blood is drink indeed. He who eats my flesh and drinks by blood abides in me and I in him. As the living Father sent me, and I live because of the Father, so those who consume me will live because of me. This is the bread which came down from heaven, not such as the fathers ate and died; those who eat this bread will live forever.

> Jesus speaks to the people of Capernaun of the symbolic internalization of his teachings, *John* 6:53-58

It is written, "Man shall not live by bread alone."

> Jesus, after fasting in the wilderness for 40 days, responds to Satan who commands him to turn a stone into bread, *Luke* 4:4

When you give a dinner or a banquet, do not invite your friends or your brothers, sisters or your kinsmen or rich neighbors, lest they also invite you in return, and you be repaid. But when you give a feast, invite the poor, the maimed, the lame, the blind, and you will be blessed because they cannot repay you. You will be repaid at the resurrection of the just.

> Jesus speaks to the Pharisees about giving without expecting anything in return, *Luke* 14:12-14

The kingdom of heaven is like treasure hidden in a field, which a man found and hid; and for joy over it he goes and sells all that he has and buys that field. Again, the kingdom of heaven is like a merchant seeking beautiful pearls, who, when he had found one pearl of great value, went and sold all that he had and bought it.

> Jesus speaks to his disciples about values, *Matthew* 13:44-46

Anyone who wishes to be first, must be last of all...
Mark: 9:35

23. HUMILITY

If any one would be first, he must be last of all and servant of all.

Jesus speaks to his disciples after they had debated on the superiority of one over the other, *Mark* 9:35

The kings of the Gentiles exercise lordship over them and those in authority over them are called benefactors. But not so with you, rather let the greatest among you become as the least, and the leader as one who serves. For which is the greater, one who sits at table, or one who serves? Is it not the one who sits at table? But I am among you as one who serves.

Luke 22:25-27

And everyone who has left houses or brothers or sisters or father or mother or wife or children or lands for my name's sake, shall receive a hundredfold, and inherit eternal life. But many that are first will be last, and the last will be first.

The divine order, *Matthew* 19:30

Abba, if it is possible, let this cup pass from me. Not my will, but Yours be done.

Exhaustion in crisis in the Garden of Gesthemane, *Matthew* 26:39

You know that those who are supposed to rule over the Gentiles lord it over them and their great men exercise authority over them. But it shall not be so among you; but whoever would be great among you must be your servant, and whoever would be first among you must be slave of all.

For the Son of Man also came not to be served but to serve, and to give his life as a ransom for many.

A disciple is not above his teacher, nor a servant above his master; it is enough for the disciple to be like his teacher, and the servant like his master.

On the same theme, *Matthew* 10:24-25

Truly I say to you, this poor widow has put in more that all those who are contributing to the treasury. For they all contributed out of their abundance, but she out of her poverty has put in everything she had, her whole living.

Jesus speaks to the scribes, *Mark* 12:43-44

What did you go out into the wilderness to behold? A reed shaken by the wind? What then did you go out to see? A man clothed in soft clothing? Behold, those who are beautifully appareled and live in luxury are in king's courts. What then did you go out to see, a prophet? Yes, I tell you, and more than a prophet…this is he of whom it is written, "Behold, I send my messenger before your face, who shall prepare the way before you."

Jesus speaks to the multitudes concerning John the Baptist, *Luke* 7:24-27

When you are invited by anyone to a marriage feast, do not sit down in a place of honor. A more eminent man than you may be invited. And he who invited you will come and say to you, "Give your place to this man," and then you will begin with shame to take the lowest place. Neither be called masters, for you have one master, the Christ. He who is greatest among you shall be your servant; whoever exalts himself will be humbled, and whoever humbles himself will be exalted.

Jesus speaks to the crowds, *Matthew* 23:10-12

114

But when you are invited, go and sit in the lowest place so that when your host comes he may say to you, "Friend, go up higher;" then you will be honored in the presence of all who sit at the table with you. For every one who exalts himself will be humbled and he who humbles himself will be exalted.

Jesus speaks in reference to the lawyers and Pharisees about humility, *Luke* 14:8-11

Two men went up into the temple to pray—one a Pharisee and the other a tax collector. The Pharisee stood and prayed like this, "God, I thank you that I am not like other men, extortioners, unjust, adulterers, or even like this tax collector. I fast twice a week, I tithe all that I get." But the tax collector, standing far off, would not even lift up his eyes to heaven but beat his breast saying, "God, be merciful to me a sinner!" I tell you, this man went down to his house justified rather than the other; for every one who exalts himself will be humbled, but he who humbles himself will be exalted.

On the same theme, *Luke* 18:10-14

All creatures...will be resolved again into their own roots.
Mary Magdalene: 4:22

24. DEATH

Those who crave to be heirs of the dead are already spiritually dead and will inherit death. Those who seek to be heirs of the living are spiritually alive and will inherit what is both alive and dead. The dead inherit nothing, yet if they inherit what is living, they will gain Eternal Life.

Philip

The souls of every human generation will die. When these people, however, have completed the time of the kingdom and the spirit leaves them, their bodies will die but their souls will be alive and they will be taken up.

Judas

Follow me…leave the dead to bury their own dead; but as for you, go and proclaim the kingdom of God. …No one who puts his hand to the plough and looks back is fit for the kingdom of God.

Jesus speaks to one who wants to follow but tells Jesus he must bury his father first, *Luke* 9:59-62

You are wrong, because you know neither the scriptures nor the power of God.

Speaking to the Sadducees who did not believe in life after death, *Matthew* 22:29

Those who say they'll die first and then rise again are mistaken. If they do not receive resurrection while alive, they'll receive nothing when they die.

Philip

Who has great faith in truth has found the real life; this one dares dying to the self to be truly alive.

Philip

Your brother will rise again. …I am the resurrection and the life; those who believe in my teachings, though they die yet shall they live, and whoever lives and believes in me shall never die. Lazarus, come out.

> The spirit of Lazarus, Martha and Mary's brother is called back to life, *John* 11:43

The heavens and the earth will roll up in your presence, and whoever is living from the living one will not see death.

> *Thomas* 111

Destroy this temple (his body), and in three days I will raise it up.

> After turning water into wine and driving the money changers out of the temple, Jesus answers the Jews who question his authority, *John* 2:19

I will destroy [this] house, and no one will be able to build it [...].

> *Thomas* 71

When the crop ripened, he came quickly carrying a sickle and harvested it. Anyone here with two good ears had better listen!

> *Thomas* 24

...you are wrong for you know neither the scriptures nor the power of God. For when they rise from the dead, they neither marry nor are given in marriage, but are like angels in heaven.

> Speaking to the Sadducees, (who did not believe in life after death), on which wife a man would be with in eternity, *Mark* 12:24-25

Truly, truly I say to you, the hour is coming, and now is, when the dead will hear the voice of the Son of God and those who hear will live. For as the Father has life in Himself, so he has granted the Son also to have life in himself, and has given him authority to execute judgment, because he is the Son of humankind. Do not marvel at this; for the hour is coming when all who are in the tombs will hear His voice and come forth, those who have done good, to the resurrection of life, and those who have done evil, to the resurrection of judgment.

Jesus answers the chief priest's accusations when he healed on the Sabbath, *John* 5:25-29

Truly, truly I say to you, unless a grain of wheat falls into the earth and dies, it remains alone, but if it dies, it bears much fruit. Those who love their lives will lose it and those who hate their life in this world will keep it for eternal life. If any one serves me, he must follow me and where I am there shall my servant be also. If any one serves me, my Father will honor him.

John 12:24-26

No one nourished by truth will die.

Philip

Have you found the beginning then, that you seek the end? For where the beginning is the end will be. Blessed is the one who stands at the beginning: that one will know the end and will not taste death.

Thomas 18

You are from beneath; I am from above. You are of this world; I am not of this world. Therefore I said to you that you will die in your sins; for if you do not believe that I am He, you will die in your sins.

Jesus speaks to the Pharisees in the treasury, *John* 8:23-24

Look for the living one as long as you live, otherwise you might die and then try to see the living one, and you will be unable to see.

Thomas 59

You will know them by their fruits.
Matthew: 7:20

25. LEADERS

No good tree bears bad fruit nor again does a bad tree bear good fruit; for each tree is known by its own fruit. Figs are not gathered from thorns, nor are grapes picked from a bramble bush. The good man out of the good treasure of his heart produces good and the evil man out of his evil treasure produces evil. For out of the abundance of the heart his mouth speaks.

> A parable from the Sermon on the Mount. We are known by our words and deeds, *Luke* 6:43-45

You would have no power over me unless it had been given to you from above.

> Jesus answers Pilot who tells him he can decide his fate, *John* 19:11

Beware that no one lead you astray saying "Lo here or lo there!" For the Son of Man is within you.

> *Mary Magdalene*, 4:34

Take heed that you are not led astray, for many will come in my name saying, "I am he!" and, "The time is at hand!" Do not go after them.

> Speaking to his disciples of self-serving leaders and prophets, *Luke* 21:8

And then if any one says to you, "Look, here is the Christ!" or "Look, there he is!" do not believe it. False Christs and false prophets will arise and show signs and wonders to lead astray, if possible, the elect. But take heed; I have told you all things beforehand.

> On the same theme, *Mark* 13:21-23

Beware of false prophets who come to you in sheep's clothing but inwardly are ravening wolves. You will know them by their fruits. Are grapes gathered from thorns, or figs from thistles? So every sound tree bears good fruit but the bad tree bears corrupt fruit. A healthy tree cannot bear corrupt fruit nor can an unhealthy tree bear good fruit. Every tree that does not bear good fruit is cut down and thrown into the fire. Thus you will know them by their fruits.

From the Sermon on the Mount, Jesus speaks to the multitudes using nature as a metaphor of life, *Matthew* 7:15-20

The Pharisees and the scholars have taken the keys of knowledge and have hidden them. They have not entered nor have they allowed those who want to enter to do so. As for you, be as sly as snakes and as simple as doves.

Thomas 39

They preach, but do not practice. They bind heavy burdens, hard to bear, and lay them on men's shoulders; but they themselves will not move them with their finger.

Speaking against religious leaders, *Matthew* 23:3-4

Let them alone; they are blind guides. And if a blind man leads a blind man, both will fall into a pit.

Concerning the Pharisees who opposed Jesus, *Matthew* 15:14

If a blind person leads a blind person, both of them will fall into a hole.

On the same theme, *Thomas* 34

And many false prophets will arise and lead many astray. And because wickedness is multiplied, love will grow cold.

Matthew 24:11-12

Simon, Simon, behold, Satan demanded to have you, that he might sift you like wheat, but I have prayed for you that your faith may not fail; and when you have turned again, strengthen your brethren.

Jesus speaks to Peter at the time of Passover, *Luke* 22:31-32

You know that those who are supposed to rule over the Gentiles lord it over them, and their great men exercise authority over them. But it shall not be so among you; but whoever would be great among you must be your servant, and whoever would be first among you must be slave of all. For the Son of Man also came not to be served but to serve, and to give his life as a ransom for many.

Mark 10:42-45

And preach as you go, saying, "The kingdom of heaven is at hand." Heal the sick, raise the dead, cleanse lepers, cast out demons. You received without pay, give without pay. Take no gold, nor silver, nor copper in your belts, no bag for your journey, nor two tunics, nor sandals, nor a staff; for the laborer deserves his food.

Jesus instructs his chosen disciples to give to others from the abundance of their spirit, *Matthew* 10:7-10

Why have you come out to the countryside? To see a reed shaken by the wind? And to see a person dressed in soft clothes, [like your] rulers and your powerful ones? They are dressed in soft clothes, and they cannot understand truth.

Thomas 78

You are the salt of the earth; but if salt has lost its taste, how shall its saltiness be restored? It is no longer good for anything except to be thrown out and trodden under foot.

Matthew 5:13

He who speaks on his own authority seeks his own glory, but he who seeks the glory of the Father is true. In him there is no falsehood.

Speaking to the Jews in the temple, *John* 7:16-18

Take heed that no one leads you astray. Many will come in my name saying "I am the one!" and they will lead many astray.

Matthew 13:5-6

False christs and false prophets will arise and show signs and wonders to lead astray, if possible, the elect.
Mark 13:22

[And they] have planted trees without fruit, in my name, in a shameful manner.
Judas

So you are Simon the son of John? You shall be called Cephas.
Jesus calls Simon his rock, *John* 1:42

When you pray, speak to your Father who is in the secret place.
Matthew: 6:6

26. PRAYER

Seek and you will find. In the past, however, I did not tell you the things about which you asked me. Now I am willing to tell them, but you are not seeking them.

Thomas 92

For where two or three are gathered in my name, there am I in the midst of them.

Matthew 18:20

Let one who seeks not stop seeking until he finds. When he finds, he will be troubled. When he is troubled, he will be astonished and will rule over all.

Thomas 2

And when you pray you must not be like the hypocrites, for they love to stand and pray in the synagogues and at the street corners that they may be seen by others. Truly I say to you, they have their reward. But when you pray, go into your room and shut the door and pray to your Father who is in secret and your Father who sees in secret will hear you. And in praying do not heap up empty phrases as the Gentiles do, For they think that they will be heard for their many words. Do not be like them for your Father knows what you need before you ask. Pray then like this:
Our Father who is in heaven, hallowed be Your name. Your kingdom come, Your will be done on earth as it is in heaven. Give us this day our daily bread and forgive us our debts as we forgive our debtors. And lead us not into temptation but deliver us from evil.

Matthew 6:5-13

Beware of practicing your piety before others in order to be seen by them. Then you will have no reward from your Father who is in heaven.

From the Sermon on the Mount, *Matthew* 6:1

Which of you who has a friend will go to him at midnight and say to him, "Friend, lend me three loaves, for a visitor has arrived on a journey and I have nothing to set before him." And he will answer from within, "Don't bother me. The door is shut now and my children are in bed. I cannot get up and give you anything?" I tell you, though he will not get up and give you anything because he is your friend, yet because of his importunity he will rise and give whatever it is that you need. And I tell you, ask and it will be given to you; seek and you will find; knock and it will be opened to you. For everyone who asks receives and he who seeks finds and to him who knocks it will be opened. What father among you, if his son asks for a fish will instead of a fish give him a serpent, or if he asks for an egg, will give him a scorpion? If you then, who are imperfect, know how to give good gifts to your children, how much more will the heavenly Father give the gift of Spirit to those who ask Him!

Jesus speaks to his followers of the importance of persistence in prayer, *Luke* 11:5-13

In a certain city there was a judge who neither feared God nor regarded man, and there was a widow in that city who kept coming to him and saying, "Vindicate me against my adversary." For a while he refused; but afterward he said to himself, "Though I neither fear God nor regard man, yet because this widow bothers me, I will vindicate her or she will wear me out by her continual coming." ...Hear what the unrighteous judge says. And will not God vindicate his elect who cry to Him day and night?

On the same theme, *Luke* 18:2-7

Truly, truly I say to you he who believes in me will also do the works that I do, and greater works than these will he do because I go to the Father. Whatever you ask in my name, I will do it that the Father may be glorified in the Son. If you ask anything in my name, I will do it.

Before he is crucified, Jesus speaks of the Creator's need to be made manifest through his creation, *John* 14:12-14

Truly, truly I say to you if you ask anything of the Father he will give it to you in my name. Before you have asked nothing in my name. Ask and you will receive that your joy may be full.

On the same theme, *John* 16:23-24

Again I say to you, if two of you agree on earth about anything they ask, it will be done for them by my Father in heaven.

Matthew 18:19

Watch and pray that you may not enter into temptation. The spirit indeed is willing, but the flesh is weak.

Jesus finds his disciples sleeping in the garden at Gesthemane, *Mark* 14:38

Pray that you may not enter into temptation.

Luke 22:40

But watch at all times, praying that you may have strength to escape all these things that will take place and to stand before the Son of Man.

Luke 21:36

This kind (of evil) cannot be driven out by anything but prayer and fasting.

The disciples ask Jesus why they did not have the power to cast out an unclean spirit, *Mark* 9:29

Ask and it will be given to you. Seek and you will find. Knock and it will be opened to you. For everyone who asks receives. And she who seeks finds and to him who knocks it will be opened.

Matthew 7:7-8

One who seeks will find, and for [one who knocks] it will be opened.

Thomas 94

What is truth?
John: 18:38

27. SPIRIT OF TRUTH

For this reason I was born. For this reason I have come into the world, that I should bear witness to the truth. Everyone who is of the truth hears my voice.

Jesus answers Pilate's question, "Are you a king?" *John* 18:37

If you love me, you will keep my commandments. And I will pray the Father and He will give you another Counselor, to be with you forever, even the Spirit of Truth whom the world cannot receive because it neither sees It nor knows It. You know It, for It dwells with you and will be in you.

Discourse at the Passover Supper, *John* 14:15-17

These things I have spoken to you while I am still with you. But the Counselor, the Holy Spirit whom the Father will send in my name, will teach you all things and bring to your remembrance all that I have said to you.

John 14:25-26

It is the spirit who gives life. The flesh profits nothing.
The words that I speak to you are spirit, and they are life.

John 7:63

Don't lie and don't do what you hate, because all things are disclosed before heaven. After all, there is nothing hidden that will not be revealed, and there is nothing covered up that will remain undisclosed.

Thomas 6

But when they arrest you and deliver you up, do not worry beforehand, or premeditate what you will speak. But whatever is given you in that hour, speak that, for it is not you who speak, but the Spirit of Truth.

Jesus speaks to his disciples, *Mark* 13:11

Now when they bring you to the synagogues and magistrates and authorities, do not worry about how or what you should answer, or what you should say. For the Holy Spirit will teach you in that very hour what you ought to say.

Jesus speaks to his disciples about the trials to come,
Luke 12:11-12

But when they deliver you up, do not worry about how or what you should speak. For it will be given to you in that hour what you should speak; for it is not you who speak, but the Spirit of your Father who speaks in you.

Matthew 10:19-20

Therefore settle it in your hearts not to meditate beforehand on what you will answer; for I will give you a mouth and wisdom which all your adversaries will not be able to contradict or resist.

Luke 21:14-15

When the Counselor comes whom I shall send to you from the Father, even the Spirit of Truth who proceeds from the Father will bear witness to me; and you also are witnesses, because you have been with me from the beginning.

John 15:26-27

When the Spirit of Truth comes, It will guide you into all the truth; for It will not speak on Its own authority, but whatever It hears It will speak, and It will declare to you the things that are to come. It will glorify me for It will take what is mine and declare it to you. All that the Father has is mine; therefore I said that It will take what is mine and declare it to you.

John 16:13-15

When all the truth is revealed then humankind may be perfected. Truth, unlike ignorance, while latent is at rest, but when revealed is stronger than the foe. It brings freedom! John wrote, "Truth will set you free."...If we know truth, its blossom will flower in our hearts and bring salvation; at the moment we're a mere appearance in creation.

Philip

But the hour is coming, and now is, when the true worshipers will worship the Father in spirit and truth; for the Father is seeking such to worship Him. God is Spirit, and those who worship Him must worship in spirit and truth.

John 4:23-24

If any one thirst let them come to me and drink. Whoever believes in me as the scripture has said, "Out of his heart shall flow rivers of living water."

The Spirit compared to water, *John* 7:37-38

Give me a drink...If you knew the gift of the Father and who it is that is saying to you, 'Give me a drink,' you would have asked and the living water would have been given to you...Every one who drinks of this water will thirst again, but whoever drinks of the water that I shall give will never thirst; the water that I shall give will become a spring of water welling up to eternal life.

Jesus speaks to a Samarian woman of new life in the Spirit,
John 4:7-14

If you continue in my word, you are truly my disciples and you will know the truth and the truth will make you free.

Jesus speaks to the believing Jews of liberty by enlightenment,
John 8:31-32

Those above revealed to those below, so we could know the mysteries of truth. This is how the truth is given; not hidden in the darkest night but revealed in brightest day of holy light!

Philip

135

But I say to you, do not swear at all: neither by heaven, for it is God's throne; nor by the earth, for it is His footstool; nor by Jerusalem, for it is the city of the great King. Nor shall you swear by your head, because you cannot make your hair white or black. But let your "yes" be "yes" and your "no" be "no." For whatever is more than these is from the evil one.
Matthew 5:34-37

For out of the abundance of the heart the mouth speaks.
Luke 6:45, *Matthew* 12:34

Therefore whoever shall confess me before men, I will also confess before my Father who is in heaven. But whoever shall deny me before men, I will also deny before my Father who is in heaven.
Matthew 10:32-33

Truth, which existed since the beginning, is sown everywhere. And many see it being sown, but few are they who see it being reaped. If we know the truth, we shall find the fruits of the truth within us. If we are joined to it, it will bring our fulfillment.
Philip

Holy Father...keep them from the evil one. They are not of the world, just as I am not of the world. Sanctify them by Your truth. Your word is truth. As You sent me into the world, I also have sent them into the world. And for their sakes I sanctify myself that they may also be sanctified by the truth.
John 17:15-19

Artwork

1. Relationship to God	*I Am*
2. Relationship to Self	*Within You*
3. Relationship to Others	*Friends*
4. Dark versus Light	**Towards the Light,* by Lauren Wallace
5. Family	*Family*
6. Mary Magdalene	*Magdalene*
7. Struggle	*Man on a Log* pastel, from a Herb Ritts photo with permission
8. Anxiety	**Andrea,* by Andrea Grumbine, MA in Fine Arts, Art therapist, New York
9. Faith	*Mother's Hands*
10. Peace	**Joy Bird* by Joy E. Hagen, artist, Seattle WA
11. Money	*The Counting House*
12. The Kingdom	*The Source*
13. Now	*Harvest*
14. Christ's Purpose	*The Multitudes*
15. War & Crisis	*Nine-Eleven*
16. Awakened Perception	*Pen and Paper*
17. Children	*Acorn and the Oak* from a photograph by Julie Orrick, Sacramento, CA

*All artwork is by Elizabeth Wallace unless noted by asterisk.

Bibliography

Bible, The New King James Version

Pagels, Elaine. *Beyond Belief: The Secret Gospel of Thomas.* New York Random House, 2003.

Jacobs, Alan. *The Gnostic Gospels.* Barnes & Noble Books, Inc. 2005.

Meyer, Marvin. *The Gospels of Mary: The Secret Tradition of Mary Magdalene, the Companion of Jesus.* Harper Collins, 2004.

Kasser, Rodolphe, Meyer, Marvin, and Gregor Wurst. *The Gospel of Judas.* National Geographic Society, 2006.

King, Karen. *The Gospel of Mary of Magdala: Jesus and the First Woman Apostle.* Polebridge Press, 2003.

NOTES

NOTES

CPSIA information can be obtained
at www.ICGtesting.com
Printed in the USA
FSOW01n0856150417
33174FS